W9-BEV-427

Editor
Mary Kaye Taggart

Editorial Project Manager
Karen J. Goldfluss, M.S. Ed.

Editor in Chief
Sharon Coan, M.S. Ed.

Illustrator
Wendy Chang

Art Director
Elayne Roberts

Cover Artist
Larry Bauer

Imaging
David Bennett

Product Manager
Phil Garcia

Cover Photos
Images ©1996 PhotoDisc, Inc.

Publishers
Rachelle Cracchiolo, M.S. Ed.
Mary Dupuy Smith, M.S. Ed.

Multiple Intelligences Activities

(Grades 5 – 8)

Author

Julia Jasmine, M.A.

Teacher Created Materials, Inc.
6421 Industry Way
Westminster, CA 92683
www.teachercreated.com
©1996 Teacher Created Materials, Inc.
Reprinted, 2000
Made in U.S.A.
ISBN-1-55734-399-3

Table of Contents

The Seven Intelligences

Introduction

The purpose of this book is to provide an easy way for you to access the theory of Multiple Intelligences (MI) and apply it in your classroom with as little additional work as possible. Every time a new theory with a memorable name appears on the educational horizon, teachers have learned to hold their collective breath until they find out what effect this new theory will have on them. Now that whole schools have adapted these methods of teaching and courses of study to put the theory of Multiple Intelligences (MI) into action, this has become a real issue.

The ability to implement MI on a daily basis in the classroom can add depth to your curriculum and meaning to the way you individualize instruction. In *Multiple Intelligences Activities*, you will have an opportunity to examine and recognize the seven intelligences as originally defined by Howard Gardner in his book *Frames of Mind*. You will become aware of the various reasons for teaching to the seven identified intelligences.

This introduction and the brief overview on pages four through six will be followed by lesson plans and activities for putting the theory of Multiple Intelligences into action.

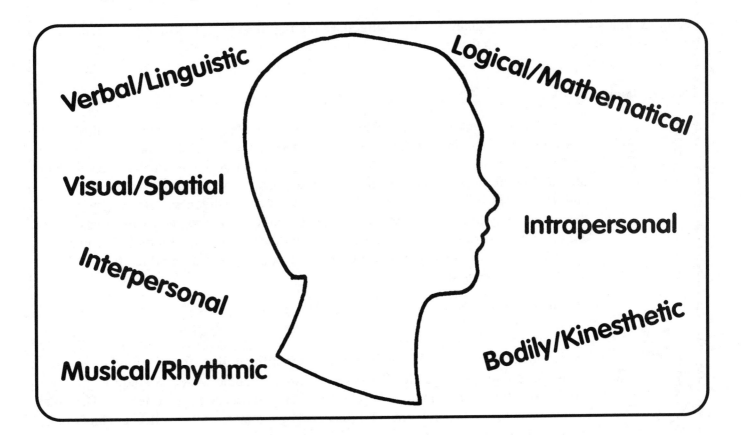

The Intelligences Described

Although he reminds us there could be many more, the seven intelligences identified by Howard Gardner in *Frames of Mind* are the following:

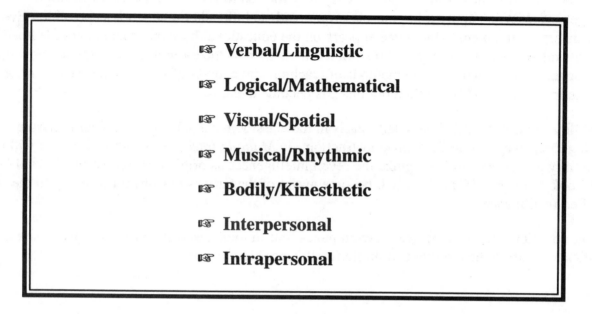

☞ **Verbal/Linguistic**

☞ **Logical/Mathematical**

☞ **Visual/Spatial**

☞ **Musical/Rhythmic**

☞ **Bodily/Kinesthetic**

☞ **Interpersonal**

☞ **Intrapersonal**

(Verbal/Linguistic and Logical/Mathematical intelligences are the most recognized, appreciated, and taught. They are the intelligences that assure success in school.)

Verbal/Linguistic

Verbal/linguistic intelligence is also called simply verbal intelligence. It is different from the other intelligences because everyone who speaks can be said to possess it at some level, although it is clear that some people are more linguistically talented than others. Verbal/linguistic intelligence expresses itself in words, both written and oral, and in auditory skills. People who have this kind of intelligence can learn by listening. They like to read, write, and speak, and they like to play with words. They are often seen as possessing high levels of the other intelligences simply because standard testing tools usually rely on verbal responses, no matter which type of intelligence is being assessed.

Logical/ Mathematical

Logical/mathematical intelligence includes scientific ability. It is the kind of intelligence that is often called "critical thinking." People with this kind of intelligence like to do things with data; they see patterns and relationships. They like to solve mathematical problems and play strategy games, such as checkers and chess. They tend to use graphic organizers both to please themselves and to present their information to others. This kind of intelligence is highly valued in our technological society.

The Intelligences Described *(cont.)*

Visual/Spatial

Visual/spatial intelligence is sometimes called visual intelligence. People with this kind of intelligence tend to think in pictures and learn best from visual presentations such as movies, pictures, videos, and demonstrations using models and props. They like to draw, paint, or sculpt their ideas and often represent moods and feelings through art. They are good at reading maps and diagrams and they enjoy solving mazes and putting together jigsaw puzzles. Visual/spatial intelligence is often experienced and expressed through daydreaming, imagining, and pretending.

Musical/Rhythmic

Musical/rhythmic intelligence is sometimes called rhythmic or musical intelligence. People with this kind of intelligence are sensitive to sounds, environmental as well as musical. They often sing, whistle, or hum while engaging in other activities. They love to listen to music; they may collect CDs and tapes, and they often play an instrument. They sing on key and can remember and vocally reproduce melodies. They may move rhythmically in time to music (or in time to an activity) or make up rhythms and songs to help them remember facts and other information. If musical/rhythmic intelligence is not recognized as a talent, it is often treated as a behavior problem.

Bodily/Kinesthetic

Bodily/kinesthetic intelligence is sometimes called simply kinesthetic intelligence. People with this kind of intelligence process information through the sensations they feel in their bodies. They like to move around, act things out, and touch the people they are talking to. They are good at both small and large muscle skills and enjoy physical activities and sports of all kinds. They prefer to communicate information by demonstration or modeling. They can express emotion and mood through dance.

Interpersonal

Interpersonal intelligence is evident in the individual who enjoys friends and social activities of all kinds and is reluctant to be alone. People with this kind of intelligence enjoy working in groups, learn while interacting and cooperating, and often serve as mediators in case of disputes, both in a school situation and at home. Cooperative learning methods could have been designed just for them, and probably the designers of cooperative learning activities as an instructional method have this kind of intelligence also.

Intrapersonal

Intrapersonal intelligence is shown through a deep awareness of inner feelings. This is the intelligence that allows people to understand themselves, their abilities, and their options. People with intrapersonal intelligence tend to be independent and self-directed and have strong opinions on controversial subjects. They have a great sense of self-confidence and enjoy working on their own projects and just being alone.

The Intelligences Described *(cont.)*

Intelligence Clusters

Everyone who is "normal" has more than one type of intelligence. Indeed, almost everyone has several types of intelligence; some people have them all, although some are more highly developed than others. Even interpersonal and intrapersonal intelligences can occur in the same person, who learns to switch back and forth as necessity demands or the opportunity presents itself. Think of the teacher who deals happily and ably with many publics—administrators, colleagues, students, parents, and the community in general—day in and day out but retreats to solitude when on vacation.

There is no evidence that intelligences come in particular patterns or that some tend to be associated with others. They come in all combinations, and it is quite easy to imagine hypothetical clusters of the seven intelligences. The person with high levels of visual and kinesthetic intelligences may become an artist. Add interpersonal intelligence to that mix, and an actor may emerge. The person who combines the verbal/linguistic and musical/rhythmic intelligences may write songs or, with the addition of kinesthetic intelligence, perform his or her own music or act in musical theater. The person who combines kinesthetic and intrapersonal intelligences may turn to a sport that stresses individual excellence, such as diving or skating. A cluster of verbal/linguistic, mathematical, and intrapersonal intelligences might be represented by the research scientist—reasoning, recording data, and preferring to be alone in the lab.

It is harder, though, to recognize one's own cluster of intelligences and harder still to recognize those that may be different from one's own in others—students, or anyone else, for that matter.

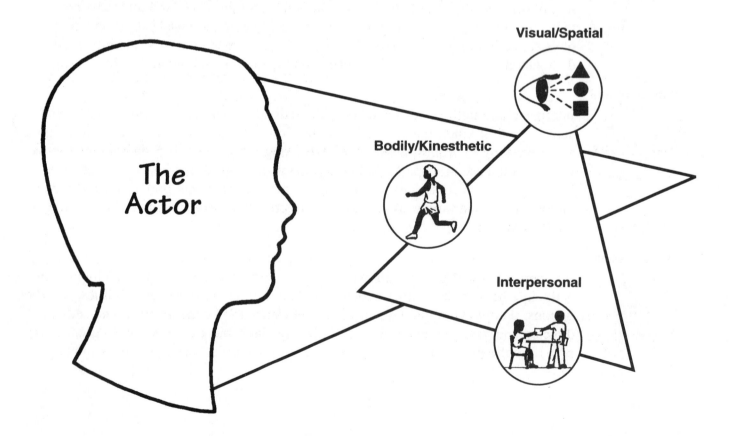

How Can They Be Identified?

Using Meta-Intelligence as a Tool

Meta-intelligence means thinking about the intelligences, just as metacognition means thinking about thinking. If you give your students enough information about how they think, they will be able to think better. If you give your students enough information about the intelligences, they will learn to identify their own strengths.

Go over the explanations of the intelligences with your students, simplifying the vocabulary as is appropriate for their grade level.

The first five intelligences refer to the ways people relate to ideas and absorb information.

- **Verbal/linguistic** means thinking in words.
- **Logical/mathematical** means thinking like a scientist.
- **Visual/spatial** means thinking in pictures.
- **Musical/rhythmic** means thinking in sounds and rhythms.
- **Bodily/kinesthetic** means thinking through touch and movement.

The last two intelligences refer to the ways people relate to themselves and each other.

- **Interpersonal** means tending to turn outward and connect with other people.
- **Intrapersonal** means tending to turn inward to explore one's own thoughts and feelings.

Relate this information to your students' everyday experiences, making the recognition of intelligences into a game.

> Everyone is a complex package of all or most of these intelligences. However, one (or more) will tend to be stronger than the others.

❆ A rock star who writes and performs his or her own songs is a combination of ______________.

(**verbal/linguistic** and **musical/rhythmic**, for sure, and probably **intrapersonal** when writing and **interpersonal** when performing)

❆ A football, baseball, or basketball player who is popular with his or her own teammates as well as with the fans is a combination of ____________________.

(**bodily/kinesthetic** and **interpersonal** and probably **visual/spatial,** because he/she would need to understand the diagrams coaches make to explain plays)

How Can They Be Identified? *(cont.)*

❀ Ricardo (a member of your class) writes pages in his journal every day but does not like to share his ideas orally or in writing.

(verbal/linguistic and **intrapersonal)**

❀ Jan (a member of your class) loves P.E., uses manipulatives to work math problems, likes to act out stories, and is always the first to volunteer to run an errand to another classroom.

(bodily/kinesthetic)

❀ Jamal (a member of your class) hums and sings to himself all day long, moves to the rhythm of any sounds, plays the drums in the school orchestra, and hides his cassette player during class but puts on earphones as soon as he leaves the room. He drives most of the teachers crazy and has a reputation as a trouble maker.

(musical/rhythmic)

Decide when your students have become comfortable with the information about the different intelligences. You can get a feeling for this by listening to see if the words have moved into their ordinary speaking vocabularies.

When one student observes another using some kind of graphic organizer and says, "Oh, you're always so visual/spatial!" or when someone reminds the class clown to sit down by saying, "Don't be so bodily/kinesthetic!" you will know that at least those students are comfortable with the concepts.

At that point you might want to try an activity like one of these:

- Have the students prioritize their intelligences by simply listing them on a sheet of paper, placing their strongest intelligence first, the next strongest second, and so on.

- Have students work in partners to prioritize each other's intelligences. Compare these lists with the first lists. Have students discuss the results: Do others see them the way they see themselves? or are there differences? Are there any big surprises? Could they consider entertaining the possibility of trying out and cultivating intelligences they don't think they possess?

- Have students use the form on page 10 or trace a circle onto a piece of paper and divide it into seven segments. The segments should be various appropriate sizes to represent the way students see the seven intelligences in themselves.

Prioritizing the Seven Intelligences

Form for Students

Name _____ Date _____

Prioritize the seven intelligences the way you see them in yourself. Put the strongest one first, the next strongest second, and so on. Then, beside the intelligences, write the ways each intelligence shows up in your life.

> - Verbal/Linguistic   • Logical/Mathematical   • Visual/Spatial
> - Bodily/Kinesthetic   • Musical/Rhythmic   • Interpersonal   • Intrapersonal

1. _____   _____

2. _____   _____

3. _____   _____

4. _____   _____

5. _____   _____

6. _____   _____

7. _____   _____

Prioritizing the Seven Intelligences

Form for Students

Name _____ Date _____

The circle below represents the total of all of your intelligences. Divide it into seven segments of various appropriate sizes, representing the way you see the seven intelligences in yourself.

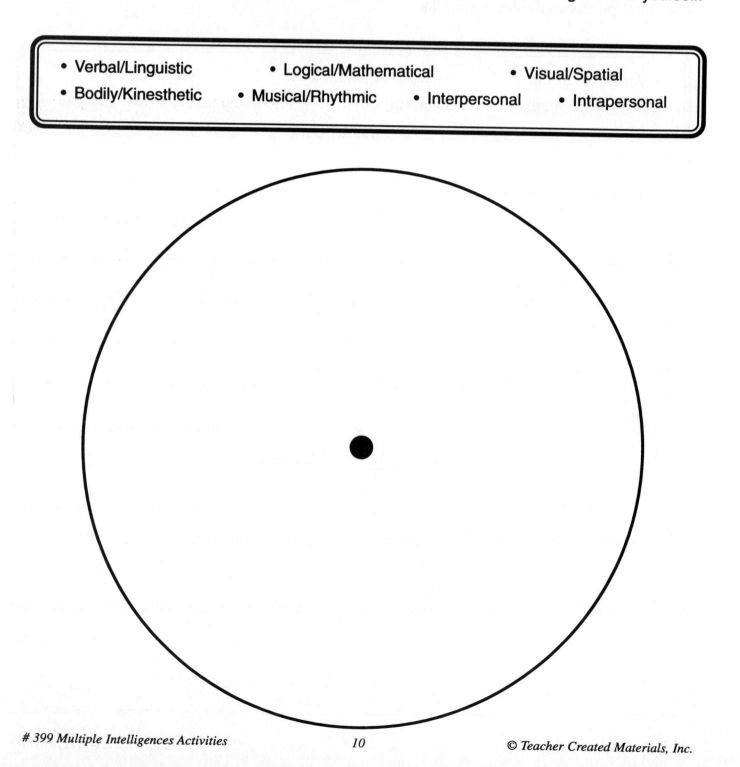

- Verbal/Linguistic
- Logical/Mathematical
- Visual/Spatial
- Bodily/Kinesthetic
- Musical/Rhythmic
- Interpersonal
- Intrapersonal

Form for Students and Teacher

Have students complete the questionnaire below (or create your own similar questionnaire). Repeat the questionnaire at regular intervals. Write your own assessment in the space at the bottom.

Multiple Intelligences

Name _____　Date _____

Write the numbers from 1 to 7 to rank the intelligences by importance to you. (1 = most important and 7 = least important)

Intelligence	Importance	Notes
Verbal/Linguistic		
Logical/Mathematical		
Visual/Spatial		
Bodily/Kinesthetic		
Musical/Rhythmic		
Interpersonal		
Intrapersonal		

Teacher's Record

Verbal/Linguistic _____

Logical/Mathematical _____

Visual/Spatial _____

Bodily/Kinesthetic _____

Musical/Rhythmic _____

Interpersonal _____

Intrapersonal _____

Sharpening Your Own Awareness

In addition to helping students identify their own strengths through the use of meta-intelligences, there are also other ways to identify and keep track of their dominant intelligences. The Teele Inventory of Multiple Intelligences (TIMI) is one of the best, as well as the easiest to use. It is short and quickly administered, so it avoids the mental meltdown associated with tests that are too long and dull. It is composed entirely of pictures, so it leaps the language barrier. However, you must learn how to ask the student who is taking it which picture of two he or she likes better or which is more like him or her. If you would like to know more about this inventory, you can contact the author.

Sue Teele, Ph.D.
Director of Education Extension
University of California, Riverside
1200 University Avenue
Riverside, CA 92507-4596
909-787-4361, Ext. 1663

You can also observe your students over a period of time and keep a checklist to document what you observe. Make your own or use one of the forms on pages 13 and 14.

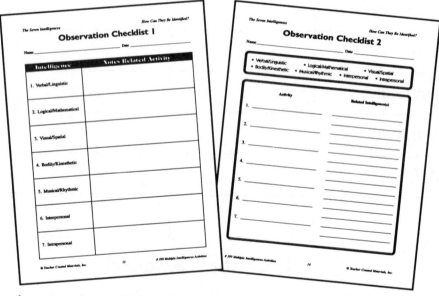

More important than inventorying and identifying, observing, and documenting is simply increasing your own awareness that everyone is different and that all of the intelligences are valuable. It is hard for anyone in our society to recognize that the less well-known and understood intelligences are equal in importance to the verbal/linguistic and logical/mathematical intelligences. And, obviously, in order to survive in our culture, everyone needs to have some competence in both of these intelligences. Teachers are especially aware of this requirement since they must prepare students for all of the kinds of official, mandated tests.

If teachers can recognize, cultivate, validate, and appreciate the other intelligences, life after formal schooling will become much richer for our society, as well as for the individuals they have taught. Research shows that while success on traditional tests, with their emphasis on the verbal/linguistic and logical/mathematical intelligences, can predict success in school, it cannot predict success in life. Schools need to provide students with all of their options.

Observation Checklist I

Name_____ Date _____

Intelligence	Notes/Related Activity
1. Verbal/Linguistic	
2. Logical/Mathematical	
3. Visual/Spatial	
4. Bodily/Kinesthetic	
5. Musical/Rhythmic	
6. Interpersonal	
7. Intrapersonal	

Observation Checklist 2

Name_____ Date _____

- Verbal/Linguistic
- Bodily/Kinesthetic
- Logical/Mathematical
- Musical/Rhythmic
- Visual/Spatial
- Interpersonal
- Intrapersonal

Activity	**Related Intelligence(s)**
1. _____	_____
	_____
2. _____	_____
	_____
3. _____	_____
	_____
4. _____	_____
	_____
5. _____	_____
	_____
6. _____	_____
	_____
7. _____	_____
	_____

Why Should They Be Taught?

Many Reasons

There are many reasons for addressing multiple intelligences in your classroom. Once you have determined the intelligences of the students in your class, you can enrich and cultivate each individual's dominant intelligences, remediate and strengthen the weaker ones, or just allow everyone to experience all of them.

There is some controversy about these choices. Some people feel that students will develop spontaneously in their areas of strength and should, therefore, be helped to develop their weaker areas. Other people stress the importance of facilitating the flowering of the dominant intelligences. Still others feel that all areas should be cultivated in everyone, no matter what the natural strengths and weaknesses.

Aren't They Natural Talents?

An argument can be made that the less well-recognized intelligences, those other than the verbal/linguistic and logical/mathematical, are really talents that will eventually appear naturally in those students lucky enough to be born with them. To a certain extent this is probably true, but many times these talents may remain latent, never discovered or discovered much later in life, because they were not triggered by experiences.

However, if an individual is placed in an environment that is rich in all kinds of intellectual and sensory stimuli, he or she may have what Howard Gardner calls a "crystallizing" experience. This can be a life-changing event. Gardner discusses Menuhin, the violinist, who first heard the violin played at the age of three and never lost his passion for it. Although not everyone will have such a dramatic experience, many students will discover interests and capabilities that will last throughout their lives.

The kind of rich environment that nurtures crystallizing experiences is particularly important for very young children because it gives them such an early start. Nevertheless, older children, as well as adults, can benefit from this kind of environment too. Think of someone like Grandma Moses who was exposed to painting very late in life and became famous for her work in that medium.

What About the Real World?

It is a fact that our society demands competence in the first two intelligences, verbal/linguistic and logical/mathematical. We would be cheating our students if we did not help them to get ready for life in the real world of tests and academic achievement. But this emphasis does not need to preclude the other intelligences. Many schools are meeting all of these needs. Let's take a look at how they are doing it.

What About Assessment?

Can the Intelligences Be Assessed?

We know for sure that the verbal/linguistic and logical/mathematical intelligences can be assessed because we do it all the time. All of the standard tests assess either through language—oral or written—or through mathematical notation combined with language. Both IQ tests and achievement tests are language based; if a student's intelligence lies elsewhere, he or she might not get into college and may never find out that he or she is very talented in some area that is not as highly valued by society.

But, can the other intelligences identified by Gardner—visual/spatial, bodily/kinesthetic, musical/rhythmic, interpersonal, and intrapersonal—be assessed? And, if so, how can this be done without filtering the assessment through language, logic, and mathematics? Gardner urges the use of assessment that is "intelligence-fair." Assessment that is intelligence-fair must be such that an intelligence can be judged directly and not through the medium of another intelligence.

What Instruments Can Be Used?

What testing instruments and procedures do we have now that will lend themselves to intelligence-fair assessment? Most of the so-called "new" or alternative assessments can be adapted for this purpose. Used in this way, they will, of course, still be subject to the same criticisms they are facing now.

Critics of alternative assessment methods say they are not "reliable." Reliable assessment can be defined as assessment that is consistent, no matter who scores it. This has always been true for normed tests, tests that were tried out on a representative population and standardized to produce percentiles, grade-level equivalencies, and letter grades—all of which could be used for purposes of comparison. The people who believe that reliability, as defined above, is all-important seem to be saying that teachers need an outside authority to validate all measurements of progress. They are also saying, whether they mean to or not, that all testing must be done objectively, through the verbal/linguistic or logical/mathematical intelligences.

Alternative assessment is not objective. In fact, it is subjective. It uses instruments such as observations verified by checklists and anecdotal records and portfolios with rubrics and reflections. It is not exact. Its application may vary from place to place, school to school, teacher to teacher, and student to student. It is a tool for measuring student performance on an ongoing basis. It can be used to make recommendations about steps that should be taken both in school and at home to ensure future progress, an area of concern that Gardner feels has been long neglected in favor of norming or ranking.

Application in the Classroom

Although Gardner recommends and does research on intelligence-fair assessment, he looks at the process from the point of view of a psychologist. It is up to educators to take this information and apply it in a way that is consistent with what actually goes on in a school. Teachers are necessarily aware of their accountability both to their administrators and, increasingly, to the parent and taxpayer communities. So, what are the tools that are presently available, and how can teachers use them to assess the seven intelligences and still meet their professional responsibilities? Let's look at the instruments mentioned above—observations verified by checklists and anecdotal records and portfolios with rubrics and reflections.

What About Assessment? *(cont.)*

Observation

We have already taken a look at observation as a method of identifying students' intelligences. Observation in a classroom for purposes of assessment sounds easier than it is. Anyone with some experience and empathy can look around a classroom and see what is going on, but in order to be used as an assessment tool, observation must be structured, documented, and repeated at regular intervals.

Observation can be structured by being linked to specific activities. For example, you might decide to formally observe your cooperative groups to determine their levels of performance in the area of interpersonal intelligence. After thinking this through, you would design an easy-to-use checklist representing the goals you want your groups to reach.

You would then document your observations by using the checklist you designed and repeat this process once a month or once a quarter or at whatever intervals work for you. This process will give you a consistent record of progress over a period of real time.

The Seven Intelligences   *What About Assessment?*

Observation

This is an example of how to use a checklist to document your observations of an individual student's use of the multiple intelligences.

Checklist for Multiple Intelligences—Sample

Name *Chung Park* Date *2/18*

Task *Acquire knowledge about ethnic holiday celebrations*

Intelligence	Demonstrated
Verbal/Linguistic	Wrote essay comparing American and Chinese New Year
Logical/Mathematical	Used graph to organize statistics about number of people celebrating various holidays
Visual/Spatial	Designed paper lantern decoration
Bodily/Kinesthetic	Showed class how to make paper lantern decoration
Musical/Rhythmic	Played tape from home—traditional Chinese holiday music
Interpersonal	Showed class how to make paper lantern decoration (see bodily/kinesthetic)
Intrapersonal	Read books about ethnic holidays silently to herself at every opportunity

© *Teacher Created Materials, Inc.*   23   *# 399 Multiple Intelligences Activities*

Checklists

The checklist mentioned so casually above is not as easy and self-explanatory as it may sound. It is, of course, a list of things to be checked off by the observer. But what things? We have all gotten into the habit of depending on objective, multiple-choice tests designed to measure incremental, and usually minimal, proficiency skills to tell us what our students know. For instance, many reading tests measure knowledge of phonics. A good reader—someone who can read words and comprehend their meanings—who learned to read by generalizing from a sight vocabulary might easily fail a phonics test.

Check Chart for _____

Marty	Ben	Maria	Gabe	Tam	Vince	Danny
?	√ −	+	?	− − −	+ +	
Julie	Mary	Fran	Robert	Jenny	Marilyn	Carl
?	+	+ + +	+ + ? + + + + + +	+ −	? ?	
Pam	Luan	Betsy				
+ +	+ +	− ?				
				David	Tuan	Liz
				+ +	+ + +	− + ?
				Roger	Mario	Terri
				+ +	− + +	? ? ?

Key

? = student has a question	√ = participation
+ = correct response	− = needs individual attention

What About Assessment? *(cont.)*

Checklists *(cont.)*

In order to make a meaningful checklist, you must do a task analysis. Figure out what really goes into the achievement of a particular goal. For example, what characteristics and accomplishments really represent interpersonal intelligence in a group situation? Put in the things that are important and leave out those that are irrelevant. Try out your checklist a couple of times before you decide to base your whole assessment system on it. Development of a good checklist is worth the time you will need to put into it. (See the Task Analysis and Checklist forms and samples on pages 20–26.)

Anecdotal Records

Observations can also be documented through the use of anecdotal records. Anecdotal records used to be lists of comments stated objectively and used to document behavior problems. The new style of anecdotal records are positive comments that document the development and growth of students. They depend on teacher interpretation and judgment and focus on the things students can do, not what they cannot do. Anecdotal records can be kept on ordinary paper, but it is convenient to have special forms that will remind you to note the names and dates of your observations. (See Sample Anecdotal Records and Anecdotal Record Forms on pages 28–31.)

Date	Student's Name	Comment
3/14/94	Peter Matthews	Moved to back of room so he could concentrate—new maturity?
3/14/94	Marty Myers	No homework again—she mentioned something going on at home—maybe conference later
3/15/94	José Lopez	All he can talk about is the track meet this afternoon—changed conference to tomorrow

Portfolios

Portfolios can be thought of as containers in which to gather and store all of the records generated by the new methods of assessment. They can also be thought of as an assessment method which provides a way to take a look at and compare work in order to observe progress over a period of time. Portfolio assessment is most often thought of in connection with written work (thus documenting the products of the verbal/linguistic and logical/mathematical intelligence); however, it is just as possible to collect, store, and compare video and audio tapes documenting products of the visual/spatial, bodily/kinesthetic, musical/rhythmic, and interpersonal intelligences. Art objects, athletic activities, dance and musical performances, and group activities, such as debates are all examples that come to mind.

Reflections

Reflections are a form of self-assessment. They engage the intrapersonal intelligence, the hardest intelligence to see in action. Reflections were originally developed for, and have been associated with, the writing process. They are, however, equally adaptable to any other work that has been completed by a student.

What About Assessment? *(cont.)*

Reflections *(cont.)*

They can be removed from the written emphasis of the verbal/linguistic domain by allowing students to reflect orally using a tape recorder and documenting the oral account with photographs. If students have personal tapes stored in their portfolios, they can rewind, listen to what they previously recorded, and consider the progress they have made before making new comments. (See Reflection Forms on pages 32–33.)

Rubrics

Rubrics are a useful addition to the assessment toolbox. The word "rubric" literally means "rule." When used in connection with assessment, a rubric is a scoring guide based on the requirements that were established to differentiate among the degrees of competency displayed in completing a task.

Once upon a time rubrics were secret documents hidden away by the teacher or by the district testing office and brought out only to grade the writing samples that determined whether a student would pass or fail or even graduate. Today, however, rubrics are shared with and even developed by students. They are no longer developed just for writing samples, but can be constructed for any task. A student who is generating a writing sample or any other product should have free access to the rubric which describes the standards by which the finished work will be judged. (See Sample Rubrics and Rubric Forms on pages 36–38.)

Translation

The last assessment tool is sometimes called "translation." It is a technique in which information taken in through one intelligence is put out through another. Students using this technique are often delighted to find that they have knowledge they had never been able to put into words. You might ask your bodily/kinesthetic students to dance their summary of a poem or mime their understanding of a rule. Or, let your students with visual/spatial intelligence paint their impressions of a piece of music or draw what the other side of a pictured object would look like.

A checklist could undoubtedly be constructed to document the observation of this technique, but it is entirely subjective for both student and teacher and might better be left as an experience of personal growth and expression.

Examples

Examples of assessments tailored to fit specific ways of teaching the intelligences are included in each of these four sections:

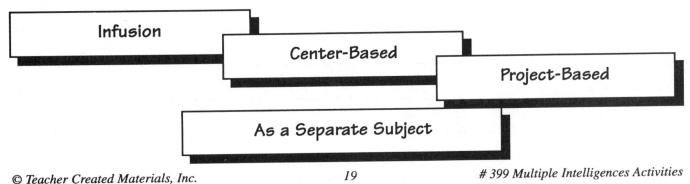

Infusion

Center-Based

Project-Based

As a Separate Subject

Selecting a Task

Use these questions to help you decide on a task to prompt your observation-based assessment. Add more questions if you wish.

Questions to Ask Yourself

Task Being Considered

_____

_____

Questions

1. Does this task match my instructional goals? Which ones?

_____

_____

_____

_____

2. Will the completed task reflect the skills and knowledge I want my students to acquire? What are they?

_____

_____

_____

_____

3. Are several intelligences represented in the task? Which ones?

_____

_____

_____

_____

_____

_____

Describing the Task

Use these questions to help you describe the task you chose. Add other questions that are important or relevant to you.

Questions to Ask Yourself

Task Being Considered

_____

_____

Questions

1. How will the material be presented to the students? Which intelligences will be involved?

_____

_____

_____

_____

2. Will the work be done by cooperative groups or by individuals?

_____

_____

_____

3. What materials will I need? List them here.

_____   _____

_____   _____

_____   _____

_____   _____

_____   _____

Creating Intelligence-Fair Assessment

Use these questions to help you describe intelligence-fair assessment for the task you chose. Add other questions that are important or relevant to you.

Questions to Ask Yourself

Task Being Considered

_____

_____

Questions

1. What responses will I expect from the students? Will they create products?

_____

_____

_____

_____

2. What will my standards be for an excellent response? . . . an acceptable response? . . . a poor response?

_____

_____

_____

_____

3. How does completion of this task relate to my instructional goals? to district/state goals?

_____

_____

_____

_____

_____

_____

Observation

This is an example of how to use a checklist to document your observations of an individual student's use of the multiple intelligences.

Checklist for Multiple Intelligences—Sample

Name _Chung Park_   Date _2/18_

Task _Acquire knowledge about ethnic holiday celebrations_

Intelligence	How Demonstrated
Verbal/Linguistic	Wrote essay comparing American and Chinese New Year
Logical/Mathematical	Used graph to organize statistics about number of people celebrating various holidays
Visual/Spatial	Designed paper lantern decoration
Bodily/Kinesthetic	Showed class how to make paper lantern decoration
Musical/Rhythmic	Played tape from home—traditional Chinese holiday music
Interpersonal	Showed class how to make paper lantern decoration (see bodily/kinesthetic)
Intrapersonal	Read books about ethnic holidays silently to herself at every opportunity

Observation

Use this form to document your observations of an individual student's use of the multiple intelligences as applied to the topic of your choice.

Checklist for Multiple Intelligences—Form

Name_____ Date _____

Task _____

Intelligence	How Demonstrated
Verbal/Linguistic	
Logical/Mathematical	
Visual/Spatial	
Bodily/Kinesthetic	
Musical/Rhythmic	
Interpersonal	
Intrapersonal	

A Simple Method for Checking Almost Anything

Checklists do not have to be complicated. This is a simple method of checking almost anything, including students' understandings of difficult concepts and their participation in class discussions.

You will need a large piece of paper divided into squares or rectangles. A large desk-pad calendar is perfect for this. Use this like a seating chart, writing in the names of the students in their approximate seat locations. If you have multiple classes, you can have a seating chart for each of your classes. Keep the charts stacked on your desk. Be sure to label them clearly (Period Two—Math) so you do not grab the wrong one by mistake.

Make a simple key. If you are observing a class discussion, you can use a plus (+) for a correct response, a minus (-) for a response that reflects a need for individual instruction, a question mark for a student's question, and so on.

You can see in the completed chart below that Marty asked a question, Tam needed some help, and Robert dominated the discussion by giving eight correct responses.

Check Chart for _____

Marty	Ben	Maria	Gabe	Tam	Vince	Danny
?	√ –	+	?	– – –	+ +	
Julie	Mary	Fran	Robert	Jenny	Marilyn	Carl
?	+	+ + +	+ + ? + + + + + +	+ –	? ?	
Pam	Luan	Betsy				
+ +	+ +	– ?				
				David	Tuan	Liz
				+ +	+ + +	– + ?
				Roger	Mario	Terri
				+ +	– + +	? ? ?

Key

? = student has a question	√ = participation
+ = correct response	– = needs individual attention

If you do not have a large calendar, you can use the blank charts on page 26 or enlarge them to suit your space.

A Simple Method for Checking
Almost Anything *(cont.)*

Check Chart for _____

Check Chart for _____

Anecdotal Records and the New Assessment

Old-Style Anecdotal Records

Anecdotal records used to be lists of comments stated factually and objectively without teacher interpretation or judgment. These lists were kept by teachers who were trying to document behavior problems that were disruptimg their classrooms. They were designed to stand alone.

> 11/22: 4th Period—Bill tripped Dave with Ed's crutch.
>
> 11/23: 2nd Period—Bill opened the door and yelled at a friend. It was his period for math class.
>
> 11/25: 4th Period—Bill tore up his test and threw it on the floor.

Armed with this list, the teacher would ask the principal or the school counselor for help in dealing with a difficult student.

New-Style Anecdotal Records

Although the old-style anecdotal record may still exist, the term has been transferred into the realm of portfolio assessment and has taken on a new meaning.

Anecdotal records, new-style, are positive comments that document the development and growth of students. They depend on teacher interpretation and judgement and deal with what students can do, not what they cannot do. They may deal with interactions between students and their classwork, students and other students, or students and adults.

> 12/5: Terri did her research project on working conditions for children in Third World countries. She was able to synthesize the information from three sources and summarize it in her own words.
>
> 12/7: Terri's improved group skills were evident today in the way she listened and responded to the opinions of others in her group.
>
> 12/8: Terri explained her concerns about student council meetings to the teacher/advisor without getting angry or upset.

Comments like these are kept on lists of one kind or another and then filed in portfolios. Some teachers like to keep running lists including many students and then transfer these comments to a notebook with pages for each individual student. Other teachers would rather carry a notebook with a page for each student and flip to the appropriate page and make an entry. When the page is full, it can be filed in the student's portfolio and a new page put in the notebook. Forms supporting both methods are provided on pages 28–31.

Anecdotal Records/Classroom List—Example

This is an example of how to keep a running classroom list of observed behaviors. The comments are written with the idea of being transferred to individual forms and may be elaborated upon at the end of the day.

Record of Observed Behavior

Date	Student's Name	Comment
3/14/94	Peter Matthews	Moved to back of room so he could concentrate—new maturity?
3/14/94	Marty Myers	No homework again—she mentioned something going on at home—maybe conference later
3/15/94	José Lopez	All he can talk about is the track meet this afternoon—changed conference to tomorrow

Anecdotal Records/Classroom List

Run off several copies of this form and carry them around on a clipboard to make moment-by-moment comments on what you observe in your classroom. Transfer the comments to individual record forms, elaborating as desired, at the end of the day.

Record of Observed Behavior

Date	Student's Name	Comment

Anecdotal Records/Individual—Example

This is an example of how to keep an individual record of observed behaviors. One of these pages is made for each student and kept in alphabetical order in a three-ring binder for convenient access. When the page is filled up, it can be replaced with a new page and the filled page placed in the student's portfolio.

Individual Anecdotal Record

Name ___*José López*___   ___*Period 3*___

Date	Comment
10/10/94	*Doing well in history—all of a sudden he has a new interest. Planning new contract.*
10/15/94	*All he can talk about is the track meet this afternoon. I changed the conference to tomorrow.*
10/16/94	*Hooray! He won! Now he can talk about history. He agreed to quite a demanding contract. He may wind up with an A this semester.*

Anecdotal Records/Individual

Run off several copies of this form and keep them (one for each student in your class) in a three-ring binder. Make your notes right on the appropriate form. When a page is filled up, it can be replaced with a new page and the filled page placed in the student's portfolio. No time will be lost transcribing information!

Individual Anecdotal Record

Name _____

Date	Comment

Reflections

This form is designed to assist you in reflecting on a single piece of your own work. Reflecting on a piece of work means looking at it in order to make a thoughtful response to it.

Reflecting on a Piece of Work

Name _____ Date _____

Description of Work

_____

_____

_____

I chose to reflect on this piece of work because _____

_____

_____

_____

It shows my growth in these intelligences: (Circle those that apply.)

VERBAL/LINGUISTIC

LOGICAL/MATHEMATICAL

VISUAL/SPATIAL

BODILY/KINESTHETIC

MUSICAL/RHYTHMIC

INTERPERSONAL

INTRAPERSONAL

If I were to redo this piece now, I would _____

_____

_____

_____

Reflections *(cont.)*

This form is designed to assist you in reflecting on your general progress over a period of time.

Reflecting on Progress

Name _____ Date _____

During _____ I made progress in the use of these intelligences: (Circle those that apply.)

> **VERBAL/LINGUISTIC**
>
> **LOGICAL/MATHEMATICAL**
>
> **VISUAL/SPATIAL**
>
> **BODILY/KINESTHETIC**
>
> **MUSICAL/RHYTHMIC**
>
> **INTERPERSONAL**
>
> **INTRAPERSONAL**

This improvement can be noticed because _____

_____

_____

_____

During the next _____

_____

I plan to work on _____

_____

_____

_____

_____

_____

_____

Do-It-Yourself Directions: A Personal Rubric Workshop

Most ready-made rubrics were created to reflect the writing process. You can, however, design your own rubric to assess whatever you want, in this case, one or more of the multiple intelligences.

Why Would I Want to Write a Rubric? (I'm Trying to Teach!)

There are several reasons for wanting to write a rubric of your own:

1. You know what you have been teaching.
2. You know what you expect your students to have mastered.
3. You know what separates excellent and average achievement from achievement that needs remediation.
4. Ready-made rubrics do not reflect your curriculum or your expectations.
5. If you are involved in teaching IDUs (Interdisciplinary Units), it would be appropriate to build into your rubric, and the prompt it represents, a variety of skills and concepts reflecting all of the academic areas with which you are working.

How Do I Begin?

First, it is important to know that your prompt and rubric are part of the same package.

Second, it is vital to realize that this is an interactive procedure—you will write, try out, and revise your prompt/rubric package until it tells you what you really want to know. Getting it right the first time is a result of years of experience or plain luck!

Write the Rubric First

It is probably easier to write the rubric first. If you review the level at which your students are working and isolate the skills you want them to have, you are well on your way. A three-point rubric is easiest, and you can begin at any point.

The three points parallel one another and reflect different levels of the same skills. The HIGH PASS contains all of the features of the PASS, either in identical form or as a more advanced variation. The NEEDS REVISION score considers parallel features, but they may be expressed as negatives.

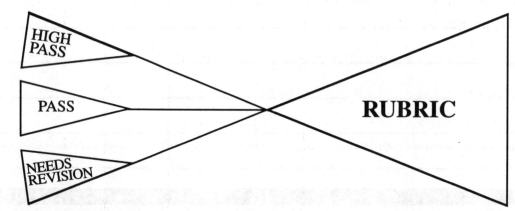

Do-It-Yourself Directions: A Personal Rubric Workshop *(cont.)*

When you write your own rubric and decide on the skill(s) and/or concept(s) to be assessed, you will also decide on what, for you, would be acceptable performance, and that will be your PASS. You will decide on the level of expertise that would exceed "average" expectations and make that your HIGH PASS. Then you will decide on the characteristics of a sample that would keep it from passing and write that variation in the section called NEEDS REVISION. Once you have decided on a skill or concept to include in your rubric, it must appear in some form in all of the points.

Write the Prompt

Your prompt should be written to elicit a response that will allow assessment of the points in your rubric. (For an example of a prompt, see page 36.) If your HIGH PASS requires the students to use sensory/descriptive words that appeal to all of the senses you should not instruct them to use sensory/descriptive words that appeal to some of the senses. This seems obvious, but sometimes you will not catch this kind of thing until you are reading a batch of papers. If you suddenly realize that you are not getting any high papers, you may want to look back at the wording of your prompt.

Revise, Revise, Revise

There are many reasons to consider revising your rubric and/or prompt. Look for some of these:

---

1. No high papers

⇨   **Did I require something I have not taught?**

⇨   **Did I require something in the rubric I did not ask for in the prompt?**

2. All high papers

⇨   **Did I place my expectations too low?**

⇨   **Did I want this result? (It is possible, and often desirable, for everyone to do really well.)**

3. No passing papers

⇨   **Were the directions wrong or easy to misinterpret?**

⇨   **Was the format different from our usual lessons?**

4. Results inconsistent with the way I see my class

⇨   **Do I need to look at the prompt-rubric package?**

⇨   **Do I need to take another look at the class?**

Student Prompt—Sample

This is an example of how to create a student prompt for an interpersonal task script.

Prompt for a Student Response

Teacher Script

Teacher says: Today you will have an opportunity to show me how you work in a cooperative group. Read the directions to yourself as I read them aloud.

1. Group Skills

Organize your group by . . .

. . . reading the assigned task (below).

. . . choosing and assigning appropriate group roles.

. . . dividing up the work.

2. Work Skills

Approach the task by . . .

. . . working quickly and efficiently.

. . . fulfilling your assigned role.

. . . completing your share of the task responsibly.

. . . organizing the data in an original way.

. . . preparing a group presentation.

3. Social Skills

Facilitate the task by . . .

. . . making positive comments.

. . . conducting polite discussions.

. . . allowing the group to reach consensus.

Task: Compare and contrast the cities of New York and Los Angeles in the areas listed below:

• location
• climate
• size in population
• size in area
• original settlers

Organize your data in an interesting way and be ready to present it to the class.

Do-It-Yourself Student Prompt for an Interpersonal Task—Sample

This is an example of how to create a student prompt for an interpersonal task. When you present a prompt to your class, ask your students to read the directions to themselves as you read them out loud.

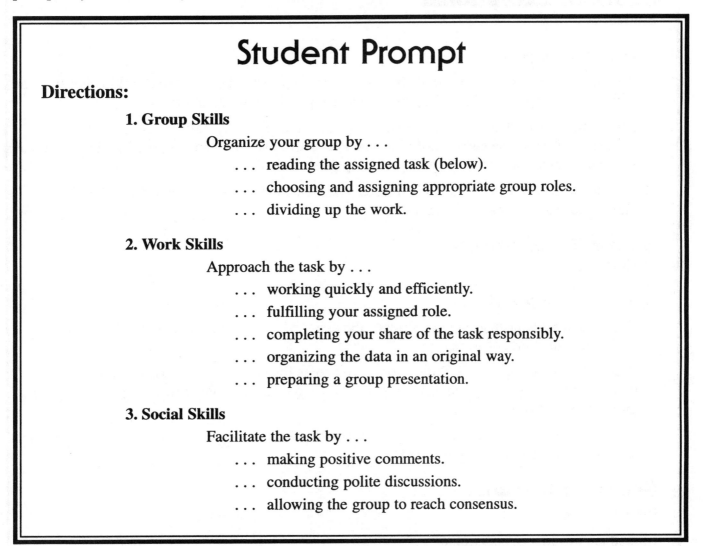

Student Prompt

Directions:

1. Group Skills

Organize your group by . . .

    . . . reading the assigned task (below).

    . . . choosing and assigning appropriate group roles.

    . . . dividing up the work.

2. Work Skills

Approach the task by . . .

    . . . working quickly and efficiently.

    . . . fulfilling your assigned role.

    . . . completing your share of the task responsibly.

    . . . organizing the data in an original way.

    . . . preparing a group presentation.

3. Social Skills

Facilitate the task by . . .

    . . . making positive comments.

    . . . conducting polite discussions.

    . . . allowing the group to reach consensus.

Task: Compare and contrast the cities of New York and Los Angeles in the areas listed below:

- location
- climate
- size in population
- size in area
- original settlers

Organize your data in an interesting way and be ready to present it to the class.

Scoring Rubric—Sample

This is an example of how to create a rubric for an assigned task.

Score 3: Exceptional
Student . . .

. . . responds to the prompt

. . . demonstrates excellent group skills (reads the assigned task, takes an active part in choosing and assigning appropriate group roles, takes an active part in dividing up the work).

. . . demonstrates excellent work skills (works quickly and efficiently, fulfills assigned role, completes share of the task responsibly, takes an active part in organizing the data in an original way, takes an active part in preparing a group presentation).

. . . demonstrates excellent social skills (makes positive comments, conducts polite discussions, allows the group to reach consensus).

Score 2: Adequate
Student . . .

. . . responds to the prompt.

. . . demonstrates adequate group skills (reads the assigned task, accepts assigned role, accepts his/her assigned part of work).

. . . demonstrates adequate work skills (works with some distraction, fulfills assigned role, completes share of the task, helps in organizing the data in an original way, helps in preparing a group presentation).

. . . demonstrates adequate social skills (makes mostly positive comments, takes part in discussions, allows the group to reach consensus).

Score 1: Minimal
Student . . .

. . . may not respond to the prompt.

. . . demonstrates limited group skills (may not read the assigned task, does not accept assigned role or assigned part of work).

. . . demonstrates inadequate work skills (does not stay focused, does not fulfill assigned role or complete share of the task, does not help in organizing the data or in preparing group presentation).

. . . demonstrates inadequate social skills (makes negative comments, does not take part in discussions, interferes with group efforts to reach consensus).

Score 0: No Response

Prompt for a Student Response

Use this blank form to create a script for prompting a student response. Choose your own intelligence-related task.

Teacher Script

Teacher Says: Today you will have an opportunity to show me . . .

_____

_____

_____

Read the directions to yourself as I read them aloud.

_____

_____

_____

_____

_____

_____

_____

Task: _____

_____

_____

_____

_____

_____

Student Prompt

Use this blank form to create a student prompt for an assigned task.

Student Prompt

Directions:

_____

_____

_____

_____

_____

_____

_____

_____

_____

_____

Task:

_____

_____

_____

_____

_____

Scoring Rubric

Use this blank form to create a rubric for an assigned task.

Score 3: Exceptional
Student . . .

Score 2: Adequate
Student . . .

Score 1: Minimal
Student . . .

Score 0: No Response

Ways to Teach and Assess the Multiple Intelligences

Can the Intelligences Be "Taught"?

So how exactly does one share this new knowledge, this new way of seeing the world? You can explain the intelligences to people, of course. You can list them, define them, and describe them. You can show students how to think about the intelligences because meta-intelligence (discussed in a previous section), like metacognition, gives people power. But can you actually teach the intelligences in the sense of helping someone to attain a particular one?

Where Shall We Start?

Howard Gardner, who originated the idea of MI, writes from the point of view of a psychologist. He would like to see an upheaval and reorganization of the whole school system. He sees the ideal school as a place where individual students will have their intelligences recognized and fostered, where they will be placed in a position to use those intelligences, and where their achievements will be evaluated in the context of the same intelligences.

Educators, however, are not in the business of waiting for utopia. While there might be some agreement with the idea that the whole educational structure needs to be torn down and built again from the ground up, we will start with several less dramatic solutions to this problem because, even allowing for the necessity of working within the context of large class sizes, inadequate supplies and facilities, and traditional methods of assessment, almost any philosophy can be implemented by determined and dedicated teachers.

Many Methods Are Being Used Successfully

Since Gardner has never tried to tell anyone how to apply his theory, schools and districts all over the country are experimenting with different approaches to teaching MI. These approaches are designed to fit particular circumstances—a school in one area may redesign the whole curriculum based on giving equal time to each of the seven intelligences, while a school in another area may keep its traditional base of verbal/linguistic and logical/mathematical instruction and "add on" experiences in the other intelligences. Each of these approaches has its enthusiastic supporters, as do all of the variations that lie in between. Basically, it seems reasonable to do whatever suits you, your students, and your community.

Some Examples

There are two basic ways to teach the intelligences through the curriculum: They can be taught as a subject in their own right—"straight" or undiluted, as it were—or infused into the regular curriculum. There are also interesting variations and combinations. Two approaches that we will look at are Center-Based and Project-Based instruction.

Ways to Teach and Assess the Multiple Intelligences *(cont.)*

Examples Defined

Infusion

❖ For this method of instruction you take an area of the curriculum (or a theme or an objective) and devise an approach that would involve each of the intelligences.

❖ In this approach you move from the curriculum out into the intelligences.

❖ Infusion can be exceptionally successful, as shown in the special "masterpiece" lesson that follows.

Advantage: It does not add another area to the curriculum.

Disadvantages: It can be insignificant and arbitrary.
It demands continuous and innovative planning.

Center-Based

❖ Curriculum is based on a theme.

❖ Centers are keyed to intelligences.

Advantages: Centers can be ongoing.
Activities tend to build on one another.

Disadvantages: Initial preparation is extremely time consuming.
Scheduling is complex.

Project-Based

❖ This resembles the "jigsaw" method of cooperative learning.

❖ Each student responds differently to the same topic.

Advantages: Each intelligence can be met and enriched.
Assessment can be intelligence-fair.

Disadvantages: There can be no expectation that students will experience the entire topic.

As a Separate Subject

❖ This is a method of instruction in which you take one (or more) of the intelligences and demonstrate it in such a way that an environment will be provided to support a crystallizing experience.

❖ In this approach you move from the intelligences out into the curriculum.

❖ This method allows for archetypal experiences.

Advantages: Material will not be forced, artificial, or insignificant.
This method will automatically involve the processes of meta-intelligence.

Disadvantages: It adds another area to the curriculum.

Infusion

Infusing the Intelligences into the Curriculum

If you want to keep teaching your regular curriculum without adding another area to your lesson plans, you can endeavor to make sure that all, or as many as possible, of the intelligences are infused into every lesson. Since the infusion should be meaningful, this is not as easy to do as it may look at first glance. However, some of the intelligences are easier to infuse than others and some curricular areas are easier than others to manipulate.

The "Masterpiece" Lesson: a Classic Example

In "Multiple Intelligences: Seven Ways to Approach Curriculum," an article which appeared in *Educational Leadership**, Thomas Armstrong writes about a lesson that has already become a classic. He details his experiences in creating and teaching a lesson in telling time (logical/mathematical) for first graders. He started by telling an exciting and original story (verbal/linguistic) about the O'Clocks, an Irish family with 12 children who lived in the Land of Time. The children (named One, Two, and so on) in this family announced the time hourly with a catchy little rhyme (musical/rhythmic). After hearing the whole story, the first graders took turns standing in front of a huge, handless clock and acting out the roles of the O'Clock children who, incidentally, each had one tiny hand and one huge hand (bodily/kinesthetic). The first graders then went on to play more clock games (interpersonal) with numbers, dance around to the tune of "Rock Around the Clock" (bodily/kinesthetic and musical/rhythmic), and write original stories (verbal/linguistic and intrapersonal) illustrated with clock faces (visual/spatial).

This is a curriculum-based lesson that includes (and includes again!) all of the intelligences in a dramatic and playful way. Who would not love to teach this way? But most teachers do not have time to make every one of the infusion lessons they will teach on a day-to-day basis into this kind of a masterpiece.

If you are teaching in a self-contained classroom, you will need to infuse the intelligences into your whole curriculum—language arts, mathematics, social studies, science, art, physical education, and music—and you will need to do this every day.

Verbal/linguistic intelligence is usually well covered, and it is easy to check off interpersonal if you use cooperative learning. Most teachers can come up with a logical/mathematical application and invent an art activity for visual/spatial. But what about the others? You can begin to cope by adopting a standard lesson plan form and reducing your expectations to a reasonable level.

Give yourself a margin for success by striving to include at least five of the intelligences in each lesson and all of them at least twice a day. See the samples and blank forms on pages 45–56 for lesson plans, tally sheets, and suggested intelligence-fair assessments.

*Armstrong, T. (1994). Multiple intelligences: Seven ways to approach curriculum. <u>Educational Leadership</u>. 52(3), 26–28.

Sample Lesson Plan One

Subject Area or Theme: *U.S. History*

Objective: *Students will be able to list sequentially, and differentiate among the wars in which the U.S. has been involved.*

Intelligences	L	L/M	S	B/K	M	Inter	Intra
Over the period of a week (or longer, if needed) students will review material and . . .							
. . . meet together in cooperative groups to develop strategies for remembering the sequence of the wars in which the U.S. has been involved. *(Interpersonal)*						✓	
. . . design and create a mural showing distinguishing features of the periods in which the wars occurred. *(Visual/Spatial)*			✓				
. . . learn a song representative of the period in which a war occurred. *(Musical/Rhythmic)*					✓		
. . . learn a dance representative of the period in which a war occurred. *(Bodily/Kinesthetic)*				✓			
. . . gather data about some aspect of the wars (e.g., countries involved, casualties, length, etc.) and then organize the data in a graph. *(Logical/Mathematical)*		✓					
. . . reflect on the values represented by the opposing sides in the conflicts. *(Intrapersonal)*							✓
. . . write a piece in which you portray the values represented by the opposing sides in one or more of the conflicts. Any genre may be used. *(Verbal/Linguistic)*	✓						

Sample Lesson Plan Two

Subject Area or Theme: *Reading/Writing*

Objective: *Students will read a story about pioneers during the Westward Movement and respond in writing in the form of a journal.*

Intelligences	L	L/M	S	B/K	M	Inter	Intra
Over the period of a week (or longer, if needed) students will read material and . . .							
. . . working independently, pretend to be pioneers and keep journals that reflect the historical period of the trip. *(Intrapersonal and Verbal/Linguistic)*	✓						✓
. . . figure out how far the pioneers traveled during the whole trip and as a daily, weekly, and/or monthly average and trace the trip on a map. *(Logical/Mathematical and Visual/Spatial)*		✓	✓				
. . . working in a cooperative group, create a mural of the trip on a section of the bulletin board. *(Interpersonal and Visual/Spatial)*			✓			✓	
. . . build a model of a covered wagon, alone or in a group. *(Bodily/Kinesthetic and Interpersonal or Intrapersonal)*				✓		✓	✓
. . . working in a cooperative group, research, learn, rehearse, and perform for the class one of the songs sung by the pioneers. *(Interpersonal and Musical/Rhythmic)*					✓	✓	

Sample Lesson Plan Three

Subject Area or Theme: *Math*

Objective: *Students will use word problems to investigate math concepts.*

Intelligences	L	L/M	S	B/K	M	Inter	Intra
Over the period of a day (or longer, if necessary) students will . . .							
. . . work individually *(intrapersonal)* to write problems *(verbal/linguistic)* about math concepts *(logical/mathematical)* currently being studied, including, but not restricted to, _____ _____ _____ _____	✓	✓					✓
. . . work together, using manipulatives, to solve the problems that were created by other students. *(Interpersonal and Bodily/Kinesthetic)*				✓		✓	
. . . create illustrations to clarify their problems. *(Visual/Spatial)*			✓				
. . . work together or independently to write at least some problems about counting the beat in music. For example, how many half notes are in a bar of sheet music with a given time signature? *(Musical/Rhythmic)*					✓		

Sample Lesson Plan Four

Subject Area or Theme: *Science*

Objective: *Students will investigate the function of the pores of a leaf as it relates to photosynthesis.*

Intelligences	L	L/M	S	B/K	M	Inter	Intra
Over the period of time needed for the investigation, students will read about photosynthesis and . . .							
. . . be able to answer questions about these facts: *(Verbal/Linguistic)*	✔						
The word photosynthesis means using the energy from light to make food (photo refers to light and synthesis refers to making food.)							
Trees take in water through their roots and carbon dioxide through their leaves. By using light energy from the sun, trees change these substances into food called glucose. The gas called oxygen is given off in the process.							
. . . speculate about what would happen if the pores in leaves were closed. *(Intrapersonal)*							✔
. . . working in a cooperative group, discuss, plan, and carry out an experiment to test their ideas. *(Logical/Mathematical, Interpersonal, and Bodily/Kinesthetic)*		✔		✔		✔	
. . . draw sketches of their experiment at regular intervals. *(Visual/Spatial)*			✔				

Lesson Plan Form

Use this form to keep track of the intelligence areas covered in your lesson plans.

Subject Area or Theme:

Objective:

Intelligences	L	L/M	S	B/K	M	Inter	Intra

Sample Weekly Tally Sheet

List some of your week's most important lesson plans. Evaluate which intelligences will be used in each lesson. At the bottom of the page, total your students' exposure to each intelligence area for the week.

Week of_____

Objectives	L	L/M	S	B/K	M	Inter	Intra
1. Students will be able to list sequentially, and differentiate among, the wars in which the U.S. has been involved.	✓	✓	✓	✓	✓	✓	✓
2. Students will read a story about pioneers during the Westward Movement and respond in writing in the form of a journal.	✓	✓	✓✓	✓	✓	✓✓✓	✓✓
3. Students will use word problems to investigate math concepts.	✓	✓	✓	✓	✓	✓	✓
4. Students will investigate the function of the pores of a leaf as it relates to photosynthesis.	✓	✓	✓	✓		✓	✓
5.							
6.							
7.							
8.							
9.							
Totals	**4**	**4**	**5**	**4**	**3**	**6**	**5**

Weekly Tally Sheet Form

List some of your week's most important lesson plans. Evaluate which intelligences will be used in each lesson. At the bottom of the page, total your students' exposure to each intelligence area for the week.

Week of_____

Objectives	L	L/M	S	B/K	M	Inter	Intra
Totals							

Suggested Assessments—Sample Lesson Plan One

Subject Area or Theme: *U.S. History*

Objective: *Students will be able to list sequentially, and differentiate among, the wars in which the U.S. has been involved.*

Activities	Suggested Assessments
Over the period of a week (or longer, if needed) students will review material and . . .	
. . . meet together in cooperative groups to develop strategies for remembering the sequence of the wars in which the U.S. has been involved. *(Interpersonal)*	• Share and discuss strategies with the whole class. Demonstrate how they work.
. . . design and create a mural showing distinguishing features of the periods in which the wars occurred. *(Visual/Spatial)*	• Share and appreciate the completed mural. Decide whether or not the details look authentic.
. . . learn a song representative of the period in which a war occurred. *(Musical/Rhythmic)*	• Perform a song. Teach it to the class.
. . . learn a dance representative of the period in which a war occurred. *(Bodily/Kinesthetic)*	• Perform a dance. Tell where and when it was performed historically.
. . . gather data about some aspect of the wars (e.g., countries involved, casualties, length, etc.) and then organize the data in a graph. *(Logical/Mathematical)*	• Display and explain graphs. Tell how data was derived.
. . . reflect on the values represented by the opposing sides in the conflicts. *(Intrapersonal)*	• Present a summary of values for the class to reflect upon.
. . . write a piece in which you portray the values represented by the opposing sides in one or more of the conflicts. Any genre may be used. *(Verbal/Linguistic)*	• Read aloud written pieces or pass them around for the class to read.

Suggested Assessments—Sample Lesson Plan Two

Subject Area or Theme: *Reading/Writing*

Objective: *Students will read a story about pioneers during the Westward Movement and respond in writing in the form of a journal.*

Activities	Suggested Assessments
Over the period of a week (or longer, if needed) students will read material and . . .	
. . . working independently, pretend to be pioneers and keep journals that reflect the historical period of the trip. *(Intrapersonal and Verbal/Linguistic)*	• Discuss the experience of keeping a journal. Share its contents if you want to.
. . . figure out how far the pioneers traveled during the whole trip and as a daily, weekly, and/or monthly average and trace the trip on a map. *(Logical/Mathematical and Visual/Spatial)*	• Use a map to demonstrate how the distance traveled was figured. Compare results and averages with other students.
. . . working in a cooperative group, create a mural of the trip on a section of the bulletin board. *(Interpersonal and Visual/Spatial)*	• Discuss and appreciate the mural. Talk about the experience of working as a group. How was the leader chosen? How were decisions made?
. . . alone or in a group, build a model of a covered wagon. *(Interpersonal or Intrapersonal and Bodily/Kinesthetic)*	• Compare the model to pictures of real covered wagons. Tell how the model was constructed.
. . . working in a cooperative group, research, learn, rehearse, and perform for the class one of the songs sung by the pioneers. *(Interpersonal and Musical/Rhythmic)*	• Perform the song(s) individually or in groups. Entertain other classes that are studying the same time period.

Suggested Assessments—Sample Lesson Plan Three

Subject Area or Theme: *Math*

Objective: *Students will use word problems to investigate math concepts.*

Activities	Suggested Assessments
Over the period of a day (or longer, if necessary) students will . . . . . . work individually *(intrapersonal)* to write problems *(verbal/linguistic)* about math concepts *(logical/mathematical)* currently being studied, including, but not restricted to _____ _____ _____ _____	• Give the problems to other students to solve.
. . . work together, using manipulatives to solve the problems that were created by other students. *(Interpersonal and Bodily/Kinesthetic)*	• Explain and discuss the use of manipulatives to solve problems. Did they help you? . . . everyone? . . . some people?
. . . create illustrations to clarify their problems. *(Visual/Spatial)*	• Exchange papers and look at the drawings. Do they help to explain the problems?
. . . work together or independently to write at least some problems about counting the beat in music. For example, how many half notes in a bar of sheet music with a given time signature? *(Musical/Rhythmic)*	• Demonstrate the musical beat for one or more of the problems. Beat out the time with a partner. Did your rhythms match one another?

Suggested Assessments—Sample Lesson Plan Four

Subject Area or Theme: *Science*

Objective: *Students will investigate the function of the pores of a leaf as it relates to photosynthesis.*

Activities	Suggested Assessments
Over the period of time needed for the investigation, students will read about photosynthesis and . . . . . . be able to answer questions about these facts: *(Verbal/Linguistic)* The word photosynthesis means, using the energy from light to make food (photo refers to light and synthesis refers to making food.) Trees take in water through their roots and carbon dioxide through their leaves. By using light energy from the sun, trees change these substances into food called glucose. The gas called oxygen is given off in the process. . . . speculate about what would happen if the pores in leaves were closed. *(Intrapersonal)* . . . working in a cooperative group, discuss, plan, and carry out an experiment to test their ideas. *(Logical/Mathematical, Interpersonal, and Bodily/Kinesthetic)* . . . draw sketches of their experiment at regular intervals. *(Visual/Spatial)*	 • Explain photoshythesis to another member of your class. • Draw a diagram showing the process of photosynthesis. • Write your speculation on a piece of paper. Check it when you finish your investigation. • Demonstrate and explain your experiment to the class. Was your original speculation (hypothesis) correct? • Display sketches to the class.

Intelligence-Fair Assessment Form for Infusion

Use this form to plan and describe your own lesson plan activities and assessments.

Subject Area or Theme:

Objective:

Activities	Suggested Assessments

Center-Based Instruction

A Visible Approach

If you like thematic teaching and already have many centers in your classroom, taking a center-based approach to teaching the multiple intelligences will probably appeal to you. Many education conferences feature presenters who are using this approach successfully in their own classrooms. It is an approach that is more visible than any of the others. Most centers have signs that say things like "Use Your Verbal/Linguistic Intelligence Here!" or "How Visual/Spatial Are You?" This is a feature that makes your instructional strategy easily accessible to parents and administrators alike.

Usually Combined with Thematic Teaching

The center-based approach is usually combined with thematic teaching because the theme provides not only the unifying topic that holds the instructional plan together but also the subject matter and ideas for the individual centers.

The Centers Themselves

It is natural in the center-based multiple intelligences classroom to think of seven centers—one for each of the intelligences—and this will usually work well, but you may want to combine intelligences also. The centers do not necessarily need to have a single focus, although you will probably want to have a main one. Not only will each center feature an intelligence it should also offer more than one approach to the intelligence, thus affording all students a chance to succeed. (The musical/rhythmic intelligence is always the hardest to address.)

Pulling It All Together

Once the students have been given the main information about the theme, they should be scheduled to work their way through the centers. Many teachers also try to allow time during the day for students to finish any necessary center work, to keep and share a journal or log, and to work on individual projects in which the concepts learned in the centers are applied.

Preparation and Planning

The initial preparation involved in this type of classroom organization is both time consuming and challenging. Once successfully begun, however, the results tend to be cumulative because many of the centers are ongoing, and the activities tend to build on one another. If you enjoy making your students a part of the classroom process, they can take an active part in both planning and maintaining the centers. Moreover, if a team of teachers is involved in this kind of teaching, different teachers can prepare centers so the work is divided.

Sample Theme One

Subject Area or Theme: Flight

Objective: Students will gain information about the theme, increase vocabulary, and develop research and critical thinking skills.

Literature:

- *Lost Star* by Patricia Lauber. Scholastic, 1985.

- "Wilbur Wright and Orville Wright" by Rosemary and Stephen Vincent Benet. *Poetry Place Anthology*. Instructor Books, Scholastic, 1990.

Presentation of Theme

Getting Started:

Collect books and magazines about airplanes and flight. Discuss the origins of flight. Do a flight cluster on the board. Ask students how they think airplanes fly. Discuss the importance of flight and the important people in flight history like Leonardo da Vinci and Orville and Wilbur Wright. (See an encyclopedia for others.) Introduce Amelia Earhart.

Making a Connection with Literature:

Read aloud *Lost Star* by Patricia Lauber. Discuss Amelia Earhart's life. What effect did she have on flight in the United States?

Read aloud "Wilbur Wright and Orville Wright" by Rosemary and Stephen Vincent Benét.

Related Reading:

- Chadwick, Roxanne. *Amelia Earhart*. Lerner, 1987.
- Collins, David. *Charles Lindbergh*. Garard, 1978.
- Hook, Jason. *The Wright Brothers*. Bookright, 1989
- Robbis, Jim. *The Story of Flight*. Warwick, 1989.
- Rosenblum, Richard. *Wings: The Early Years of Aviation*. Four Winds, 1980.

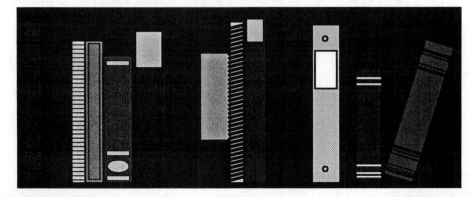

Sample Theme One *(cont.)*

Centers

Intelligences	**Activities**

Verbal/Linguistic

- Print vocabulary words associated with flight on 3"x 5" (8 cm x 13 cm) cards and have students look up words and add definitions to cards.

- Have students research, prepare, and give a two-minute oral report on a person famous in flight history.

- Have students read other poems by Rosemary and Stephen Benét and write a short report about the subjects of these poems.

Logical/ Mathematical

- Provide a chart showing the relative lengths of different types of aircraft. (See page 61.) Have students cut lengths of string to match the lengths of the airplanes and stretch them out across the playground. Label the lengths of string with the names of the planes they represent.

- Have students do a lift experiment. Provide strips of paper 2" x 10" (5 cm x 25 cm). Provide these instructions, illustrated if possible: "Using both hands, hold the strip just under your lower lip and blow." Ask students to be prepared to describe what happened, either orally or in writing.

Visual/Spatial

- Provide a diagram of an airplane. (See page 62.) Have students use an encyclopedia to label its parts.

- Provide a blank outline map of the world. (See page 63.) Have students use it to indicate the route of Amelia Earhart's around-the-world flight.

Bodily/Kinesthetic

- Have students create an airplane mobile. Use a book about airplanes or an encyclopedia to find pictures of different types of planes.

- Have students make and test paper airplanes for a paper airplane contest. The categories can be Highest Flying, Most Creative, Farthest Flying, and Longest Flying.

Sample Theme One *(cont.)*

Centers

Intelligences	**Activities**

Musical/Rhythmic

- Set up a listening post or individual tape players with earphones. Provide a tape of Symphony No. 9 in E minor *From the New World* by Antonin Dvořák. This work is often called Dvořák's *New World Symphony*. In it he uses themes from American black spirituals.

- Give students this information: In 1937, when Amelia Earhart's plane went down, there was no TV. The radio kept people informed about the unsuccessful search for her. Between the news bulletins, they played part of Dvořák's *New World Symphony*, the music that is on the tape recorder. It was the part based on a spiritual called "Goin' Home." Listen to the music and then write a paragraph describing how it made you feel.

- If you had been deciding what music to play on the radio while people searched for Amelia Earhart, would you have chosen Dvořák's *New World Symphony*? Explain. If you would have made another choice, what music would you have played? Why?

Note: Before using any outside audio or video resources, obtain the necessary school district permission.

Interpersonal

- Have students work as a group to make a sequence of events chart of Amelia Earhart's life.

- Have students prepare a list of questions they would ask if they were interviewing a pilot.

- Have each student interview another student about any experiences he or she might have had with airplanes. Students who have not flown can be interviewed about trips they would like to take.

Intrapersonal

- Have students find a book about flight and read it.

- Tell students, "Pretend you are Amelia Earhart. Make up another ending for her story."

Sample Theme One (cont.)

Chart for Logical/Mathematical Center

Aircraft	Length in Feet
Boeing 737	119
Boeing 707	153
DC Super 61	187
DC-9	120
Boeing 747	231
Concorde	193
Spruce Goose	219
Wright brothers' *Flyer I*	21
Voyager	33

Sample Theme One (cont.)

Diagram of Airplane for Visual/Spatial Center

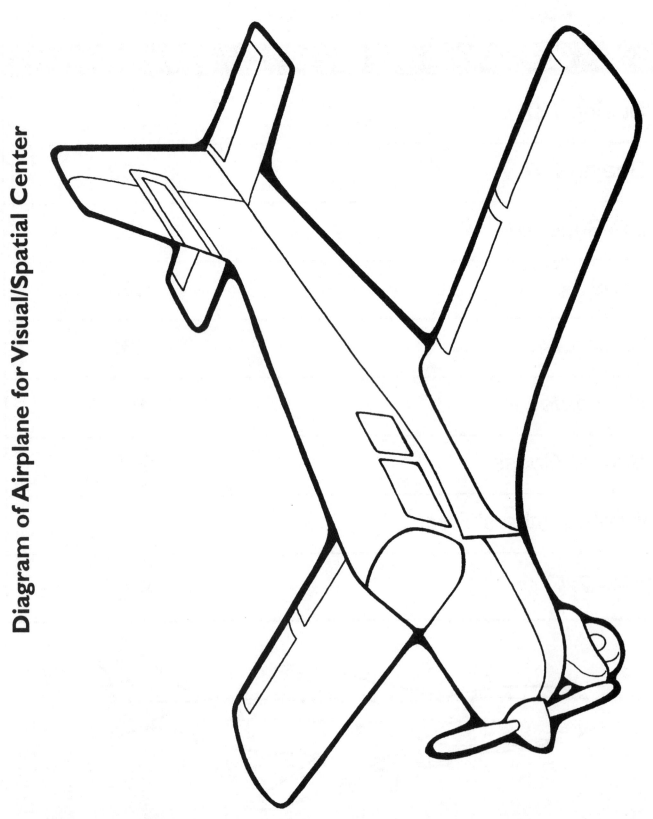

Sample Theme One *(cont.)*

Outline Map of World for Visual/Spatial Center

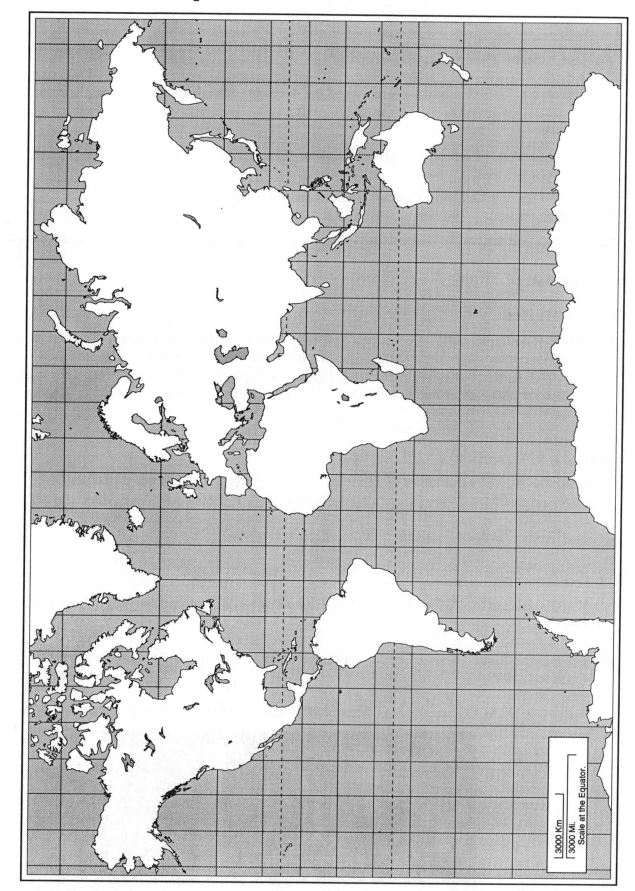

3000 Km
3000 Mi.
Scale at the Equator.

Sample Theme Two

Subject Area or Theme: *Respect/Principles*

Objective: Students will build awareness of the necessity for ethical behavior in their daily lives.

Literature:

- "Thank You, M'am," by Langston Hughes. *Relationships,* edited by Michael Spring. Scholastic, 1987.
- "Dreams" by Langston Hughes. *Reflections on a Gift of Watermelon Pickle . . .* Scholastic, 1968.

Presentation of Theme

Getting Started:

- Before reading the story ask students to think of something they really want but cannot afford to buy. Have them share their items with the class. List them on a chart. (Save the chart. See page 67.) Categorize them. (Clothing, Electronic Equipment, Entertainment, etc.) What percentage chose an article of clothing? (Have each student make a note of the item he or she chose.)

Making a Connection with Literature:

- Read the short story aloud or let students read it silently. When they are finished, ask if they were surprised that Mrs. Jones did not call the police. Ask if they would have called the authorities.

- Read aloud "Dreams," a poem by the Langston Hughes.

Related Reading:

- Hughes, Langston. "Mother to Son." *Selected Poems of Langston Hughes*. Random House, 1990.

- Williams, William Carlos. "To a Poor Old Woman." *Talking to the Sun*. Henry Holt and Company, 1995.

- Wright, Richard. "The Streets of Memphis," a chapter from *Black Boy*. Harper and Row, 1945.

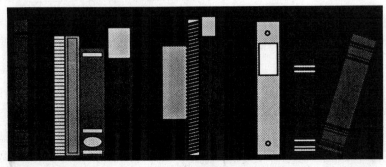

Sample Theme Two *(cont.)*

Centers

Intelligences	Activities
Verbal/Linguistic	• Students may pretend to be Roger in the story and write a letter to Mrs. Jones, explaining how he spent the money she gave him. • Students may pretend to be Roger ten years later and write a letter to Mrs. Jones, telling what has happened in his life. • Students should read other poems on this theme (see "Related Reading" on page 64) and write about them.
Logical/ Mathematical	• Provide copies of the chart on page 67. Have students estimate the cost of each item. • Provide newspaper ads, catalogues, and copies of the chart from page 67. Have students find real advertised prices for the items. • Ask students to compare their original estimates with the real prices they found. Were the real prices more or less than their estimates? What were the actual differences in prices in dollars and cents? Did anyone find more than one "real" price for an item?
Visual/Spatial 	• Ask, "What do you think Roger's neighborhood looked like? Draw a picture of it." • Say, "Draw a picture of what Roger's face looked like when Mrs. Jones gave him the money."
Bodily/Kinesthetic 	• Have students work together in groups to plan and rehearse a play based on the story. Let each group act out its play for the whole class. • Have students decide on suitable props for their plays and make them from various art materials that you supply.

Sample Theme Two *(cont.)*

Centers

Intelligences	Activities

Musical/Rhythmic

- Have at least one tape recorder with a blank tape and a microphone in the center.

- Give students this information: Langston Hughes, who wrote the short story "Thank You, M'am" and several of the poems you have read, wrote many books of poetry. The poems have been translated into at least twelve languages, and many of them have been set to music.

- Can you think of a tune for any of the poems you have read by Langston Hughes? It could be a familiar melody or one you make up yourself. You can use the microphone to tape record your idea(s).

Interpersonal

- Have students work as a group to make a chart showing important facts about various careers. They can use encyclopedias and other reference books to find out about salary, education, and availability, as well as any other information they come up with.

- Have students prepare a list of questions they would ask if they were interviewing someone about a particular career.

- Have each student make a list of questions and interview another student about his or her reaction to the story.

Intrapersonal

- Tell students to find another story by Langston Hughes and read it.

- Ask students to pretend they are Roger and make up another ending for his story.

Sample Theme Two *(cont.)*

Chart for Getting Started

Directions: Think of things you really wish you could buy for yourself. Guess how much these items cost. Then, look for advertised prices. Compare the prices.

	Category Items	Estimated Prices	Advertised Prices
Clothing			
Electronic Equipment			
Entertainment			
Other			

Sample Theme Three

Subject Area or Theme: Empathy

Objective: Students will build awareness of feelings.

Literature:

- "All Summer in a Day" by Ray Bradbury. *The Stories of Ray Bradbury*. Knopf, 1980.
- "Sunflakes" by Frank Asch. *Sing a Song of Popcorn*, selected by Beatrice Schenk de Regniers, et al. Scholastic, 1988.

Presentation of Theme

Getting Started:

- Brainstorm as a class what the world would be like with constant rain for seven years. How would it look? feel? smell? sound? How would life be different? Dim the lights and play a recording of rain showers and storms.

Making a Connection with Literature:

- Read the short story aloud, expressing, through your reading, the various moods of the story: the monotony of the constant rain, the excitement of the children, the tension of their conflict with Margot, and their fervor in the sunshine.

- Read aloud "Sunflakes," a poem by Frank Asch.

Related Reading:

- Asimov, Issac. "The Fun They Had," from *Earth Is Room Enough*. Doubleday, 1957.
- Bradbury, Ray. *The Martian Chronicles*. Doubleday, 1958.
- Walsh, Jill Patton. *The Green Book*. Farrar, 1982.
- *Children's Atlas of Earth Through Time*. Rand McNally, 1990.

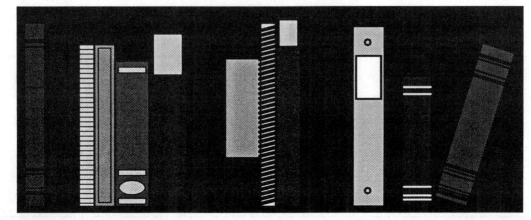

Sample Theme Three *(cont.)*

Centers

Intelligences	Activities

Verbal/Linguistic

- Students may write descriptive poems about the sun, using the couplet written by Margot as a model.

- Have students write a paragraph describing their feelings when they got something they had wanted for a long time.

- Have students write one paragraph describing their feelings when they lost something that meant a lot to them.

Logical/ Mathematical

- Have students create word problems based on the idea that the sun would shine for only one hour every seven years. For example: A child is born on February 27, 1990, two days before the sun comes. On May 6, 2004, how many times has that child seen the sun?

- Have students research the atmosphere of Venus. How does it compare with the atmosphere of Earth?

Visual/Spatial

- Provide a listening post or tape recorders with earphones and art materials, such as water colors, colored pencils, crayons, and drawing paper. Tape the passage from the story that describes the children's experience of seeing the sun for the first time. Tell students to listen to the tape with their eyes closed as they try to "see" what the children saw and then draw the picture they imagined.

- Have students refer to an encyclopedia or other reference material to draw a diagram of the solar system.

Bodily/Kinesthetic

- Have students design and make a model of the world described in Bradbury's story. (It could be as simple as a diorama.) Have them check their designs with you before they start construction.

- Have students act out Margot's reaction when she comes out of the closet.

Sample Theme Three *(cont.)*

Centers

Intelligences	Activities

Musical/Rhythmic

- Using whatever materials are available in the classroom and the center, have each small group devise ways to recreate the sounds of a rainstorm. With lights dimmed, each group can perform its storm for the class.

Interpersonal

- Have students work as a group to brainstorm reasons why the inhabitants of Earth would need or want to move to another planet. Groups can then decide if this is likely to happen.

- Have students use encyclopedias and other reference books to determine Earth's approximate population. Find out how many people can ride in the spaceships we have today. How many spaceships would be needed, under current conditions, to transport the entire population? How long would it take to get to Mars?

Intrapersonal

- Have students find another story by Ray Bradbury and read it.

- Say, "Pretend you are Margot. Make up another ending for her story."

Sample Theme Four

Subject Area or Theme: Natural Disasters

Objective: Students will build an understanding of nature and the causes of natural disasters.

Literature:

- *The Big Wave* by Pearl S. Buck. Harper and Row, 1947.

Presentation of Theme

Getting Started:

- Begin by brainstorming a list of natural disasters. The list may include hurricanes, tornadoes, volcanoes, earthquakes, monsoons, floods, and tidal waves or tsunamis.

Making a Connection with Literature:

- *The Big Wave* is a classic that can be enjoyed in one or two sittings. It should be read without interruption so that the beauty of its language and the emotion generated by the story can be fully appreciated. When the reading is completed, let students generate topics for discussion; for example, the interdependence of farmers and fishermen, how to live with dangers over which you have no control, grieving, the pros and cons of Jiya's choice to stay with Kino's family, the symbolism of Jiya's decision to put a window facing the sea into his house, etc.

Related Reading:

- Moore, Lillian. "Until I Saw the Sea." *The Random House Book of Poetry for Children.* Random House, 1983.
- Garland, Hamlin. "Do You Fear the Wind?" *Childcraft, Vol. 3.* World Book, 1987.
- Lauber, Patricia. *Volcanoes and Earthquakes.* Scholastic, 1985.

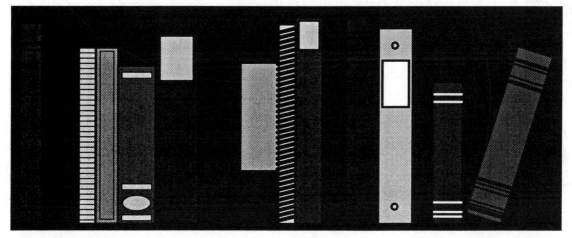

Sample Theme Four *(cont.)*

Centers

Intelligences	**Activities**

Verbal/Linguistic

- Provide examples of haiku, a Japanese verse form consisting of three unrhymed lines of five, seven, and five syllables. Haiku usually describes nature. (Examples of haiku are easily found in a library.) Have students study the examples and write a haiku of their own on the subject of natural disasters.

- Give students a definition of **personification** and some examples: **Personification is representing an idea or a thing as a person.** Examples: The west wind dances down the lane.
    The clouds are crying raindrop tears.

- Have students find examples of personification in *The Big Wave* and in the poems listed in "Related Reading" on page 71. Then have them write some of their own to describe natural happenings.

Logical/ Mathematical

- How deep is the ocean? What is a fathom? Have students research and report the answers to these questions in a graphic form.

- Have students write some word problems about natural disasters.

- Have students look up earthquakes, volcanoes, and tsunamis. What is the relationship among them? Draw and label a diagram to show their relationship.

Visual/Spatial

- Have students use the Venn diagram on page 74 to compare everyday life in Japan to life in the United States.

- Have students study terracing as a farming practice. Find pictures that illustrate this practice. What does it do? Why is it necessary?

Bodily/Kinesthetic

- Have students study the physical map of Japan on page 75. They should find and mark places where the mountains and the sea would be in the area described in the book.

- Have students make papier-mâché or salt dough maps of Japan to show its rugged topography.

Sample Theme Four *(cont.)*

Centers

Intelligences	Activities

Musical/Rhythmic

- Using whatever materials are available in the classroom and center, have each small group devise ways to express the experience of natural disasters with sound. What does an earthquake sound like? a tornado? a hurricane? a volcano? Some students may actually know, but it can be just as effective to imagine these sounds.

- Have groups perform for the rest of the class. See if the class can figure out which natural disaster is being portrayed.

Interpersonal

- Have each small group discuss one of these topics. Have them choose a leader to record their conclusions: (See page 76.)

   — the interdependence of farmers and fishermen

   — how to live with dangers over which you have no control

   — grieving

   — the pros and cons of Jiya's choice to stay with Kino's family

   — the symbolism of Jiya's decision to put a window facing the sea into his house

Intrapersonal

- Prepare reading response journals. (Reproduce page 77 or divide a piece of paper in half vertically. On one side write quotations from the book. Leave the other side blank for the students' responses.) Ask students to respond to the quotations and continue with quotations they choose themselves.

- Have students find another book by Pearl Buck and read it.

Sample Theme Four *(cont.)*

Venn Diagram for Visual/Spatial Center

United States

Japan

Sample Theme Four (cont.)

Bodily/Kinesthetic Center

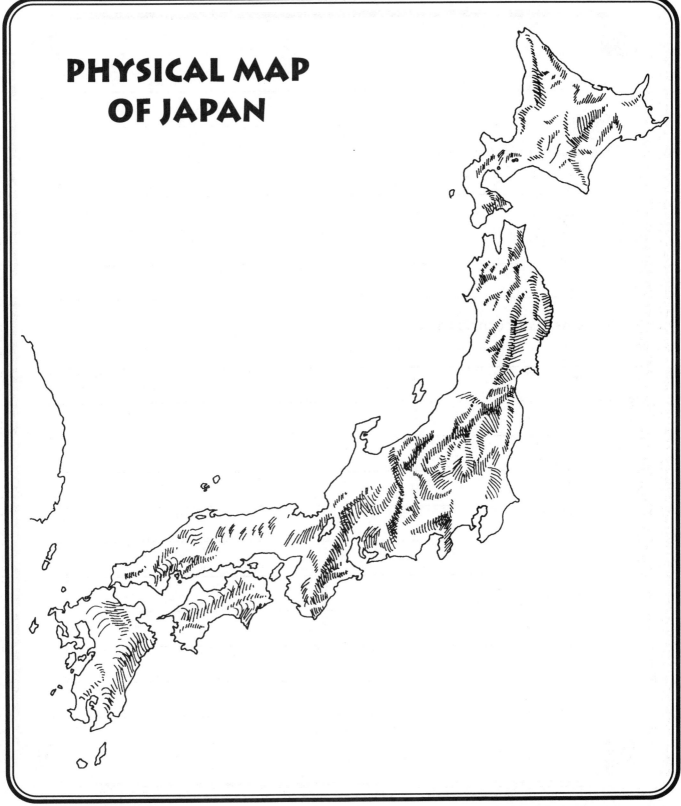

PHYSICAL MAP OF JAPAN

Sample Theme Four *(cont.)*

Form for Interpersonal Center

Group _____

Leader _____

This was our discussion topic:

_____

_____

_____

_____

These were our conclusions:

_____

_____

_____

_____

_____

_____

_____

_____

_____

_____

_____

_____

Sample Theme Four *(cont.)*

Reading Response Journal for Intrapersonal Center

Directions: Read the quotations in the left column. Write what you think each quote means in the right column.

Quotation	Response

Lesson Plan Form

Subject Area or Theme: _____

Objective: _____

_____

Literature:

- _____
- _____
- _____

Presentation of Theme

Getting Started:

- _____

_____

_____

_____

_____

Making a Connection with Literature:

- _____

_____

_____

_____

_____

_____

Related Reading:

- _____
- _____
- _____

Center Planner

Directions: Use this form and the one on the next page to plan the activities you will have available at each center.

Intelligences	Activities

Verbal/Linguistic

**Logical/
Mathematical**

Visual/Spatial

Bodily/Kinesthetic

Center Planner *(cont.)*

Intelligences	Activities
Musical/Rhythmic 	
Interpersonal 	
Intrapersonal 	

Notes: _____

_____

_____

_____

_____

Project-Based Instruction— Two Approaches

There are two types of project-based approaches being implemented in the teaching that involves multiple intelligences. There are also many variations on these two types but, basically, they can be differentiated by calling one the theme method and the other the jigsaw method.

Common Characteristic

Both methods are what might be called intelligence-fair. Howard Gardner uses this term when he discusses assessment tools that evaluate a product within the scope of the intelligence that created it. In much the same way, project-based approaches to learning allow students to explore knowledge from the vantage point of their own dominant intelligences. Thus, for example, the student who is strong in bodily/kinesthetic intelligence is not forced to write about a topic but can build something to demonstrate mastery of the subject matter.

Both methods recognize the reality of the information explosion and the fact that it is no longer possible to learn all there is to know about everything—or about anything, for that matter. The multiple intelligences approach to projects affords a different look at how we want students to learn. Simply put, not everyone will be expected to do the same things, and no one will be expected to do everything. Students choose those projects or those pieces of a project that appeal to their dominant intelligences.

The Theme Method

In the theme method a broad overall topic is selected, in some cases for a whole school. Each student is expected to create a project that will show knowledge and understanding of the subject area. When this method is used to full advantage, students are taught how to choose and develop their own projects.

Jigsaw Method

The jigsaw method bears a resemblance to the "jigsaw" method of cooperative learning originated by R. Slavin (Lyman, L., Foyle, H., & Azwell, T. *Cooperative Learning in the Elementary Classroom.* New York: National Education Association 1993). In Slavin's version various members of a group are responsible for researching different areas of an assigned topic and bringing their findings back to the group to be taught to the other members and pieced together into a whole. In responding to a multiple intelligences project, everyone participates in the same unit or theme but is free to choose the topics and/or the approaches that best suit his or her interests and talents.

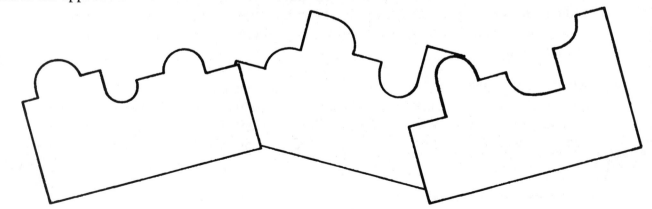

Sample of Jigsaw Method

Here are suggestions for one way to provide opportunities for students to use their intelligences in a characteristic elementary school unit on ecology. With only minor adjustments, this plan can be adapted to almost any theme or unit.

The student with *verbal/linguistic* intelligence can gather information from reference books and literature related to the topic. This student might also want to write a story or report about the topic and make an oral presentation to the class.

The student with *logical/mathematical* intelligence can collect and organize data about the subject. He or she might want to draw conclusions about the data or write math problems based on real information for the rest of the class to solve.

The student with *visual/spatial* intelligence will learn best from films, videos, maps, and graphic representations. This student may want to present his or her information in the form of a mural or a series of charts or posters.

The student with *bodily/kinesthetic* intelligence would probably enjoy doing some experiments. He or she could gather data about the amount of water used each day for one week for bathing and each day for the following week for showering and then compare the results and make some inferences about water use. This student might also enjoy making a miniature rain forest in a terrarium.

The student with *musical/rhythmic* intelligence could make musical instruments by recycling soft drink bottles (horns), wood blocks (percussion), milk cartons (rattles), and coffee cans (drums) to make an "orchestra." This student might also enjoy creating an ecology "symphony" in which other students could participate.

The student with *interpersonal* intelligence may want to move out into the community and gather information about local recycling projects. He or she could organize and communicate this information to classmates and their parents to help them know where to take their recyclable materials.

The student with *intrapersonal* intelligence might want to choose one aspect of ecology and do in depth research with an emphasis on the values connected with ecological concerns. This student might enjoy spending time in the library, working independently.

Although all of these students will be learning about ecology and probably reporting back to their classmates in one way or another, there is no expectation that anyone will learn or experience all of it. Some students will enjoy taking more than one approach, but it will be possible to succeed by completing just one activity.

Setting Standards/Assessing Results

It is essential to realize that students do not necessarily know how to select a project, often choosing topics that are either too broad or too narrow or not academic enough for school.   Once a project has been chosen, students do not necessarily know how to proceed. You want to avoid both the situation in which a student, working entirely independently, produces a project that is substandard and the situation in which a really excellent project has obviously been created by a parent at home.

Students can be given instruction in how to decide on a project. You may want to actually teach a unit on choosing and completing a project and prepare a list of projects that will address the various intelligences in the context of a given theme or instructional unit. Students also need clear criteria for success in order to set and reach goals.

Have Students Make Portfolios

Portfolios are the ideal assessment vehicle for project-based instruction. Gardner recommends video taping each student's presentation of the project and including the video tape in the portfolio.

Discuss the process of portfolio assessment with the students. Decide with them what to keep in the portfolios. Consider these questions:

- How can students keep records of projects and activities that are not on paper?

- Would they like to make video tapes? audio tapes?

- Would they like to take instant photographs?

- What standards would they like to establish for their portfolios?

This method of teaching in a multiple intelligence classroom offers excellent opportunities for increasing students' self-reliance and self-esteem. The portfolio process itself gives students control over their own learning process and a chance to reflect on their progress over a period of time.

Teaching the Intelligences as a Separate Subject (Undiluted)

Most teachers do not welcome another area added to their already crowded curriculum. Nevertheless, there are real benefits in treating the intelligences as a separate subject and moving outward from them into the curriculum.

First and most important, the material involving the intelligences will not be forced or artificial or insignificant. It can, in fact, consist of archetypes. Archetypes, according to *Webster's New World Dictionary*, are perfect examples of a type or a group. A learning environment of this kind is the ideal one to foster the crystallizing experiences described by Howard Gardner.

Secondly, dealing with the intelligences in an open and above-board manner will automatically involve the processes of meta intelligence (metacognition applied to the intelligences) with all of its benefits. This approach immediately validates students as learners who are capable of dealing with high-level subject matter.

If you decide to use this approach, you will, for at least that part of the day, be coming close to the ideal situation in which students will have direct exposure to the intelligences together with activities that will reinforce the experience.

How Can I Fit It In?

If you can find thirty to forty-five minutes per day, three days per week, three weeks per month, (a total of nine periods per month), for eight months of the year, you can teach MI as a separate subject. It merely takes a little juggling of time.

This book suggests a program schedule which is outlined on the next page. If you let September run over into October, October into November, and November into the first week of December, the rest of winter and spring is clear sailing. December is not scheduled except to pick up the overflow from November. (If you simply find the time in December to practice for the holiday program, help the students make gifts for their parents, and live until vacation, you will have done all any human being should be asked to do!)

Consult the Calendars

A calendar for the year, showing suggested days on which to plan segments one through eight, is provided on page 85. In addition, monthly calendars can be found in each segment. Use these calendars to plan the segment lessons. Of course, you will modify it as necessary for your own schedule and situation. Try to pick days and times that are relatively free from interruption and avoid usurping the time slots of other activities the students look forward to. Also, move things around any way you want. If the students are interested and you have an hour, do two periods in one day. Make two or three periods into a rainy day activity. Or, simplify an experience and use it for a sponge activity.

Calendars for the Year

September

M	T	W	T	F
	Segment 1	
	Segment 1	

October

M	T	W	T	F
	Segment 1	
	Segment 2	
	Segment 2	

November

M	T	W	T	F
	Segment 2	
	Segment 3	
	Segment 3	

December

M	T	W	T	F
	Segment 3	

January

M	T	W	T	F
	Segment 4	
	Segment 4	

February

M	T	W	T	F
	Segment 4	
	Segment 5	
	Segment 5	

March

M	T	W	T	F
	Segment 5	
	Segment 6	
	Segment 6	

April

M	T	W	T	F
	Segment 6	
	Segment 7	
	Segment 7	

May

M	T	W	T	F
	Segment 7	
	Segment 8	
	Segment 8	

June

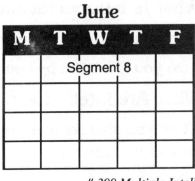

M	T	W	T	F
	Segment 8	

Segment One—Nine Lessons

From the Middle of September Through the First Week of October

During the first segment of this minicurriculum, it is a good idea to introduce the concepts and the vocabulary associated with MI. This introduction to what is actually meta-intelligences will give the students "tools" to work with as they experience each of the individual intelligences.

The topics for this segment are listed below. Pages 87 through 110 of this book will give you the information you need to review this information.

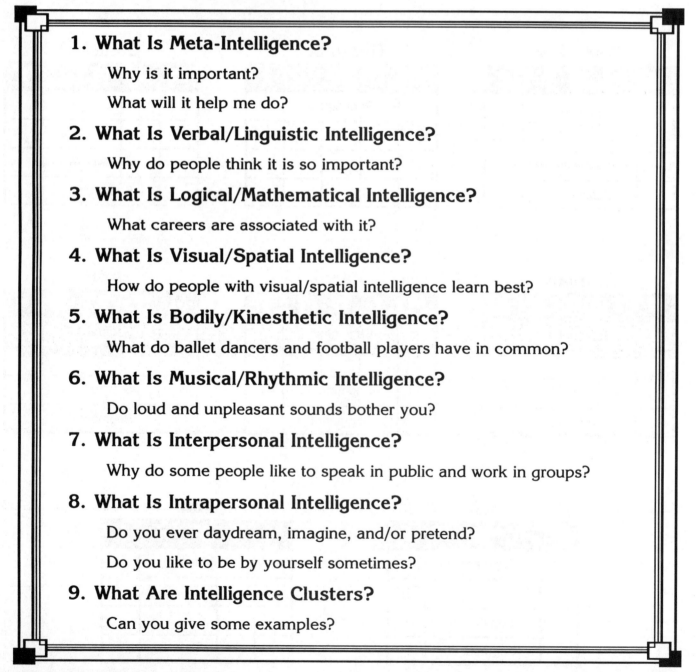

1. What Is Meta-Intelligence?

Why is it important?

What will it help me do?

2. What Is Verbal/Linguistic Intelligence?

Why do people think it is so important?

3. What Is Logical/Mathematical Intelligence?

What careers are associated with it?

4. What Is Visual/Spatial Intelligence?

How do people with visual/spatial intelligence learn best?

5. What Is Bodily/Kinesthetic Intelligence?

What do ballet dancers and football players have in common?

6. What Is Musical/Rhythmic Intelligence?

Do loud and unpleasant sounds bother you?

7. What Is Interpersonal Intelligence?

Why do some people like to speak in public and work in groups?

8. What Is Intrapersonal Intelligence?

Do you ever daydream, imagine, and/or pretend?

Do you like to be by yourself sometimes?

9. What Are Intelligence Clusters?

Can you give some examples?

Calendars for Segment One

Directions: Use the calendars below to plan when you would like to do the nine lessons of this segment. The lessons are listed on the previous page. The highlighted weeks are the time periods which are suggested.

September

M	T	W	T	F
		Segment One		
		Segment One		

October

M	T	W	T	F
		Segment One		

Segment One—Lesson One

What Is Meta-Intelligence?

Purpose: to learn about meta-intelligence, how it can be used, and why it is important

Skills: knowledge, comprehension, application, analysis, synthesis, and evaluation

Intelligences: verbal/linguistic, visual/spatial, interpersonal, intrapersonal

Materials:

- simplified graphic showing brainforming connections, one for each student
- copies of the definition on page 89, one for each student
- paper, writing materials, colored pencils, etc.
- large sheets (11" x 15" or 28 cm x 38 cm) of colored construction paper, one for each student

Procedures:

◆ Introduce this activity by passing out the definition sheet. Have students read it to themselves and then have everyone say the words aloud together and take turns reading the definitions.

◆ Pass out the graphic of the brain. Explain that scientists believe that the brain forms new electrical connections every time we take in new information. While they are learning about archetypes, meta-intelligences, and multiple intelligences, for example, their brains are forming all kinds of new connections to process and store this new information. The more they think about and discuss this information, the more complicated (and useful) the connections will be.

◆ Ask students to write a paragraph about what they just learned or design a symbol to represent it. Then, have them fold their sheets of large construction paper in half to make folders. Each student will then write his or her name on the outside of his or her folder and put the definition sheet, the brain graphic, and the paragraph or symbol into it.

◆ Collect these folders and set them aside for Segment One—Lesson Two.

To Simplify:

Stop after discussing the definition sheet and the brain graphic and do not have students write a paragraph or design a symbol.

To Expand:

Have students do research on the new discoveries being made about the brain. Watch for articles in current magazines and make them available to students. Let students report interesting information to the rest of the class.

Evaluation and Processing:

Ask students what they found most interesting and what they think will happen next. Write predictions on the board to check during the next lesson.

Segment One—Lesson One (cont.)

What Is Meta-Intelligence?

Definitions

Archetype: a perfect example of a type or group

Meta-intelligence: thinking about and studying the different ways people have of learning and relating to themselves and others

Multiple Intelligences: seven ways of relating to ideas, to ourselves, and to others; sometimes called the seven ways of being smart—they are verbal/linguistic, logical/mathematical, visual/spatial, bodily/kinesthetic, musical/rhythmic, interpersonal, and intrapersonal intelligences

Verbal/Linguistic

Logical/Mathematical

Visual/Spatial

Intrapersonal

Interpersonal

Bodily/Kinesthetic

Musical/Rhythmic

Segment One—Lesson One (cont.)

What Is Meta-Intelligence?

Brain Graphic

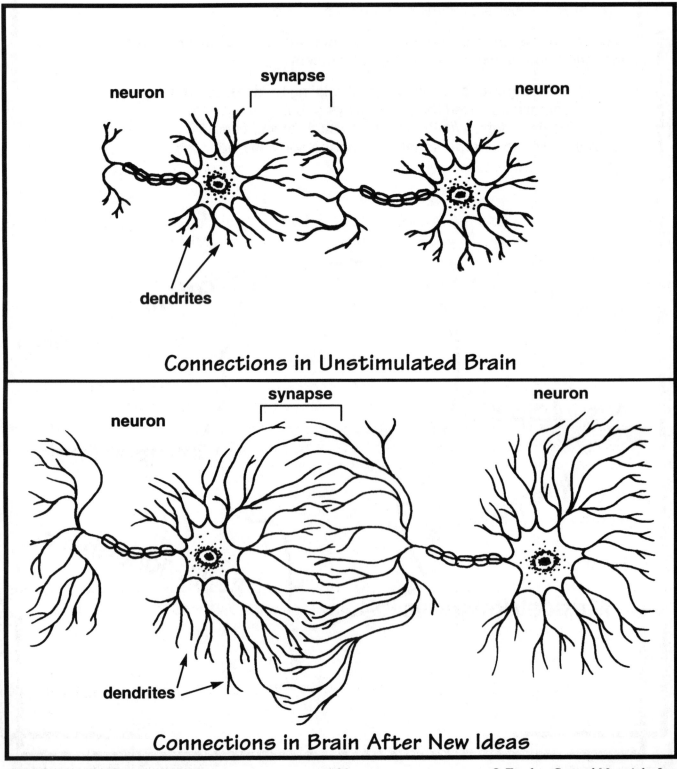

Connections in Unstimulated Brain

Connections in Brain After New Ideas

Multiple Intelligences

Segment One—Lesson Two

What Is Verbal/Linguistic Intelligence?

Purpose: to learn about verbal/linguistic intelligence, its special characteristics, and its importance in our society

Skills: knowledge, comprehension, application, analysis, synthesis, and evaluation

Intelligences: verbal/linguistic, visual/spatial, interpersonal, intrapersonal

Materials:

- copies of the definition on page 92, one for each student
- copies of "Word Games" page, one for each student
- paper, writing materials, colored pencils, etc.

Procedures:

- Introduce this activity by passing out the definition sheet. Have students read it to themselves and then have everyone say the words aloud together and take turns reading the definition. Give students time to think about and sketch their pictures or symbols.
- ◆ Discuss these ideas:
  - People who cannot hear can still communicate in words. How do they do this? How do they speak? How do they "listen"?
  - People who cannot see can still read and write. How do they "see" words? How do they "write" words?
  - Some scientists believe that our brains cannot think without using words. What do you think? Try it . . . now what? How can you tell someone else what you thought about? If you know a way, you have another kind of intelligence.
- ◆ Use the "Word Games" page, if you have time. Otherwise, use it for an extra activity or for homework. Have students store their definition papers in the folders they made in Lesson One.

To Simplify:

Use just the definition and symbol sheet.

To Expand:

Ask interested students to research American Sign Language and/or Braille and report what they learn to the class. If you have time, invite a guest to visit your class and demonstrate.

Evaluation and Processing:

Ask students what they found to be the most interesting and what they think will happen in the next lesson about mathematical/logical intelligence. Write predictions on the board to check during the next lesson.

Segment One—Lesson Two (cont.)

What Is Verbal/Linguistic Intelligence?

Definition

Verbal/Linguistic Intelligence: Also called verbal intelligence, it means thinking in words. It is different from the other intelligences because everyone who uses language to communicate can be said to possess it at some level, although it is clear that some people are more talented than others in this area. Verbal/linguistic intelligence expresses itself in words, both written and spoken, and in listening skills. People who have this kind of intelligence often like to learn by listening. They like to read and write and speak, and they like to play with words. They are often seen as having high levels of the other intelligences simply because doing well on most tests depends on the ability to read and write, no matter which type of intelligence is being assessed.

What picture or symbol could you use to remind yourself of what is meant by verbal/linguistic intelligence? Make a sketch of your idea in the space below.

Segment One—Lesson Two *(cont.)*

What Is Verbal/Linguistic Intelligence?

Word Games

List all of the games you can think of that are played with words.

_____   _____

_____   _____

_____   _____

_____   _____

Think up a word game of your own. Describe it below:

Multiple Intelligences

Segment One—Lesson Three

What Is Logical/Mathematical Intelligence?

Purpose: to learn about logical/mathematical intelligence, its special characteristics, and its importance in our society

Skills: knowledge, comprehension, application, analysis, synthesis, and evaluation

Intelligences: verbal/linguistic, logical/mathematical, visual/spatial, interpersonal, intrapersonal

Materials:

- copies of the definition on page 95, one for each student
- copies of "Inventions We Use," one for each student
- paper, writing materials, colored pencils, etc.

Procedures:

◆ Introduce this activity by passing out the definition sheet. Have students read it to themselves and then have everyone say the words aloud together and take turns reading the definition. Give students time to think about and sketch their pictures or symbols.

◆ Discuss these ideas:

  – Logical/mathematical intelligence, together with verbal/linguistic intelligence (last lesson), are considered the most important of the intelligences by many people. It is the intelligence people think brings progress. The things we use every day were invented and built by people who used this type of intelligence (combined with other kinds, of course).

  – What are graphic organizers? When you see one in a book you are reading, do you take the time to use it? Do you find graphic organizers helpful or confusing?

◆ Use the "Inventions We Use" page to finish this activity. Have students store their definition papers in the folders they made in Lesson One.

To Simplify:

Use just the definition and symbol sheet.

To Expand:

Ask interested students to name the invention that is most important to them (TV? radio? tape players? bicycles?) and try to find the name(s) of the inventor(s).

Evaluation and Processing:

Ask students what they found to be the most interesting and what they think the next really important invention will be.

Segment One—Lesson Three *(cont.)*

What Is Logical/Mathematical Intelligence?

Definition

Logical/Mathematical Intelligence: Often called "critical thinking," it means thinking like a scientist. People with this kind of intelligence like to do things with data; they see patterns and relationships. They like to solve mathematical problems and play strategy games, such as checkers and chess. They tend to use graphic organizers both to please themselves and to present their information to others. This kind of intelligence is highly valued in our technological society. (Technological means having to do with technical progress in the use of machines in industry, agriculture, and other areas.)

What picture or symbol could you use to remind yourself of what is meant by logical/mathematical intelligence? Make a sketch of your idea in the space below.

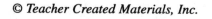

Segment One—Lesson Three *(cont.)*

What Is Logical/Mathematical Intelligence?

Inventions We Use

Think about the things you use every day. Think about the things your parents use. How many of them are run by electricity (need to be plugged in or use batteries)? On the lines below, list the things you have used so far today that were run by electricity.

_____   _____

_____   _____

_____   _____

_____   _____

_____   _____

_____   _____

Again, think about the things you use every day. Are any of them the same as the things used by your parents when they were your age? On the lines below, list the electric things you have used so far today that are just like the things your parents used at your age.

_____   _____

_____   _____

_____   _____

_____   _____

_____   _____

_____   _____

Multiple Intelligences

Segment One—Lesson Four

What Is Visual/Spatial Intelligence?

Purpose: to learn about visual/spatial intelligence, its special characteristics, and its importance in our society

Skills: knowledge, comprehension, application, analysis, synthesis, and evaluation

Intelligences: verbal/linguistic, visual/spatial, interpersonal, intrapersonal

Materials:

- copies of the definition on page 98, one for each student
- paper, writing materials, colored pencils, etc.

Procedures:

◆ Introduce this activity by passing out the definition sheet. Have students read it to themselves and then have everyone say the words aloud together and take turns reading the definition. Give students time to think about and sketch their pictures or symbols.

◆ Discuss these ideas:

   – Many people feel that in the last forty years we have become a country of people with predominantly visual/spatial intelligence. We like to think in pictures, and we like to get our information that way too. What change in our culture and/or environment is responsible for this change?

   – Do you enjoy using maps? Do you like to see where you are in relation to other places? Have you ever used a road map on a family trip? Was it fun? Was it hard or easy? Pull down a classroom map and make general observations about oceans, rivers, mountain ranges and so on. Let students point out and talk about places they have been.

◆ Have students store their definition papers in the folders they made in Lesson One.

To Simplify:

Use just the definition and symbol sheet.

To Expand:

Ask interested students to consider the question, "Which Career Do You See in Your Future?" and write about at least one career that demands visual/spatial intelligence.

Evaluation and Processing:

Ask students what they found to be the most interesting. Students who wrote about careers that require visual/spatial intelligence can share their ideas with the class.

Segment One—Lesson Four *(cont.)*

What Is Visual/Spatial Intelligence?

Definition

Visual/Spatial Intelligence: Sometimes called visual intelligence, it means thinking in pictures. People with this kind of intelligence tend to learn best from things that they see, such as movies, TV, pictures, videos, and demonstrations using models and props. They like to draw, paint, or sculpt their ideas and often represent moods and feelings through art. They are good at reading maps and diagrams, and they enjoy solving mazes and putting together jigsaw puzzles. Visual/spatial intelligence is often experienced and expressed through daydreaming, imagining, and pretending.

What picture or symbol could you use to remind yourself of what is meant by visual/spatial intelligence? Make a sketch of your idea in the space below.

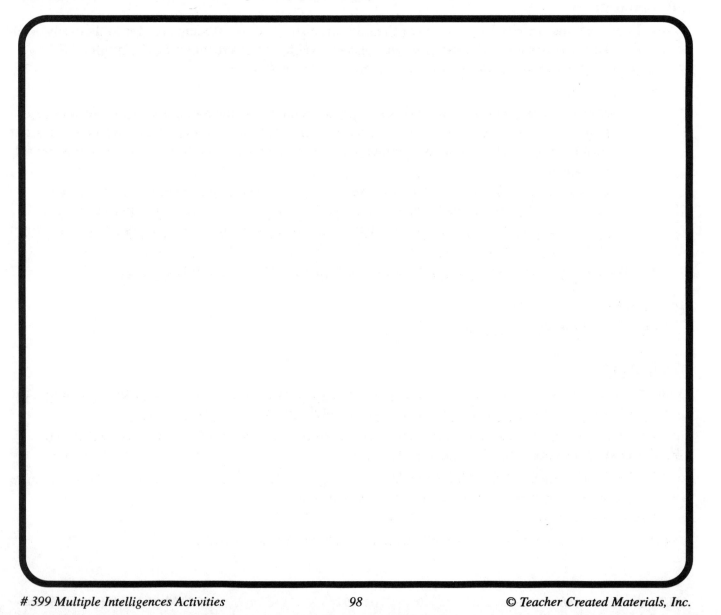

Segment One—Lesson Five

What Is Musical/Rhythmic Intelligence?

Purpose: to learn about musical/rhythmic intelligence, its special characteristics, and its importance in our society

Skills: knowledge, comprehension, application, analysis, synthesis, and evaluation

Intelligences: verbal/linguistic, logical/mathematical, musical/rhythmic, interpersonal, intrapersonal

Materials:

- copies of the definition on page 100, one for each student
- paper, writing materials, colored pencils, etc.

Procedures:

◆ Introduce this activity by passing out the definition sheet. Have students read it to themselves and then have everyone say the words aloud together and take turns reading the definition. Give students time to think about and sketch their pictures or symbols.

◆ Discuss these ideas:

  – Why is musical/rhythmic intelligence sometimes perceived as a behavior problem? Do you think it is? Where does one person's right to hear music stop and another person's right to enjoy silence start? What if the musical person is wearing earphones and no one else can hear what he or she hears?

  – Why are some rock stars treated like royalty? How much money are they paid?

  – How many of you play an instrument? . . . Have ever played one? . . . Would like to play one? . . . What is stopping you? . . . Is it too expensive? . . . Is it too much noise? . . . Do you have too many other activities?

◆ Have students store their definition papers in the folders they made in Lesson One.

To Simplify:

Use just the definition and symbol sheet.

To Expand:

Have students do some local telephone research. Show them how to use the telephone book to find and call music schools and teachers in your area. They should ask about the instruments in which instruction is offered, the instruments that are available to rent, the prices of lessons, and if there are soundproofed rooms available for practice. Students should compare their results and compile the information for display on a school bulletin board.

Evaluation and Processing:

Ask if any of the students plan to use the information about lessons. Discuss.

Segment One—Lesson Five *(cont.)*

What Is Musical/Rhythmic Intelligence?

Definition

Musical/Rhythmic Intelligence: Sometimes called rhythmic intelligence, it means thinking in sounds and rhythms. People with this kind of intelligence are sensitive to sounds in the world around them, as well as to musical sounds. They often sing, whistle, or hum while doing other things. They love to listen to music; they may collect CDs and tapes, and they often play an instrument. They sing on key and can remember and reproduce melodies with their voices. They may move in time to music (or in time to an activity) or make up rhythms and songs to help them remember facts and other information. If musical/rhythmic intelligence is not recognized as a talent, it is often treated as a behavior problem.

What picture or symbol could you use to remind yourself of what is meant by musical/rhythmic intelligence? Make a sketch of your idea in the space below.

Segment One—Lesson Six

What Is Bodily/Kinesthetic Intelligence?

Purpose: to learn about bodily/kinesthetic intelligence, its special characteristics, and its importance in our society

Skills: knowledge, comprehension, application, analysis, synthesis, and evaluation

Intelligences: verbal/linguistic, bodily/kinesthetic, interpersonal, intrapersonal

Materials:

- copies of the definition on page 102, one for each student
- copies of "A Fish Story," one for each student
- paper, writing materials, colored pencils, etc.

Procedures:

◆ Introduce this activity by passing out the definition sheet. Have students read it to themselves and then have everyone say the words aloud together and take turns reading the definition. Give students time to think about and sketch their pictures or symbols.

◆ Discuss these ideas:

    – Why are people so impressed with sports heroes? Why are they paid so much?

    – Fitness is on everyone's mind. What do you do to stay fit?

    – In a ballet, the dancers try to tell a story with their movements. Have you ever seen a ballet, either in person or on TV? Were you able to understand the story?

    – Many people use gestures (hand movements) when they talk. Do you?

◆ Finish this lesson with the "A Fish Story" activity. Discuss the results. Have students store their definition papers in the folders they made in Lesson One.

To Simplify:

Use just the definition and symbol sheet.

To Expand:

Have students research some Olympic sports in current magazines.

Evaluation and Processing:

Ask if any of the students play on teams or take lessons in dance, gymnastics, skating, martial arts, and so on. Ask what they observe about the way they and others are treated by the coaches. Discuss.

Segment One—Lesson Six (cont.)

What Is Bodily/Kinesthetic Intelligence?

Definition

Bodily/Kinesthetic Intelligence: Sometimes called simply kinesthetic intelligence, it means thinking through touch and movement. People with this kind of intelligence process information through the feelings in their bodies. They like to move around, act things out, and touch the people they are talking to. They are good at both small and large muscle skills and enjoy physical activities and sports. They prefer to communicate information by demonstration or modeling. They can express emotion and mood through dance.

What picture or symbol could you use to remind yourself of what is meant by bodily/kinesthetic intelligence? Make a sketch of your idea in the space below.

Segment One—Lesson Six *(cont.)*

What Is Bodily/Kinesthetic Intelligence?

The point of this activity is to put students in a situation where they will almost certainly "talk with their hands." You can make it more interesting by having some students put their hands behind their backs while they tell their fish story to see if they can still talk.

Cut off at the dotted line. Copy and distribute the lower part of this form to students.

- -

A Fish Story

You will be telling the other students in your class about a fish you caught. The fish can be any variety and any color, but it must be **big!**

Make up the details of your story so it sounds real. You can fish in the ocean, in a lake, or in a mountain stream. The only requirement is that your fish must be **really big!**

You may write notes in the space below to plan your story, but you will not be allowed to read it. You must tell your story without notes.

Segment One—Lesson Seven

What Is Interpersonal Intelligence?

Purpose: to learn about interpersonal intelligence, its special characteristics, and its importance in our society

Skills: knowledge, comprehension, application, analysis, synthesis, and evaluation

Intelligences: verbal/linguistic, interpersonal

Materials:

- copies of the definition on page 105, one for each student
- copies of "Group Rules," one for each group (with extras)
- paper, writing materials, colored pencils, etc.

Procedures:

◆ Introduce this activity by passing out the definition sheet. Have students read it to themselves and then have everyone say the words aloud together and take turns reading the definition. Give students time to think about and sketch their pictures or symbols.

◆ Discuss these ideas:

 – Cooperative learning groups in school give students a different way of learning. Group activities give students the opportunity to practice getting along with others, listening to the ideas they have, and expressing personal opinions in an assertive, but not aggressive, manner.

 – What is the difference between being assertive and being aggressive?

 – More and more businesses are asking their employees to work together on committees and teams. Will the cooperative group work that is done in school help people do this?

◆ Finish this lesson with the "Group Rules" activity. Use your regular groups or divide up the class in some new way. Have students store their definition papers in the folders they made in Lesson One.

To Simplify:

Use just the definition and symbol sheet.

To Expand:

Have students ask their parents if the companies they work for have them work in groups, teams, or committees. Allow time for students to report back to the class.

Evaluation and Processing:

Ask students how they feel about group work. Would they rather work in groups or alone? Does it depend on the subject or the task? Which subjects/tasks are best suited to group work?

Segment One—Lesson Seven *(cont.)*

What Is Interpersonal Intelligence?

Definition

Interpersonal Intelligence: It means tending to turn outward and connect with other people as part of the thinking process. It is expressed in the enjoyment of friends and social activities of all kinds and in not liking to be alone. People with this kind of intelligence enjoy working in groups, learn while interacting and cooperating, and often serve as peacemakers in case of disagreements, both in school and at home. They are the people who love cooperative learning groups, student council meetings, and running for office.

What picture or symbol could you use to remind yourself of what is meant by interpersonal intelligence? Make a sketch of your idea in the space below.

Segment One—Lesson Seven *(cont.)*

What Is Interpersonal Intelligence?

Group Rules

What does **consensus** mean? Write its definition below.

_____

_____

_____

_____

Meet with your cooperative learning group and decide on some rules that will make group work more productive and more enjoyable. After you decide on your rules, reach a **consensus** on the five most important ones and write them below. Be ready to discuss them with the whole class.

_____

_____

_____

_____

_____

_____

_____

_____

_____

Segment One—Lesson Eight

What Is Intrapersonal Intelligence?

Purpose: to learn about intrapersonal intelligence, its special characteristics, and its importance in our society

Skills: knowledge, comprehension, application, analysis, synthesis, and evaluation

Intelligences: verbal/linguistic, intrapersonal

Materials:

- copies of the definition on page 108, one for each student
- paper, writing materials, colored pencils, etc.

Procedures:

◆ Introduce this activity by passing out the definition sheet. Have students read it to themselves and then have everyone say the words aloud together and take turns reading the definition. Give students time to think about and sketch their pictures or symbols.

◆ Discuss these ideas:

- Which of our classroom activities appeal to people with intrapersonal intelligence? Is it possible to have both intrapersonal and interpersonal intelligences and to use them at different times and for different things?

- Is having intrapersonal intelligence the same as being shy? (Read the definition again and think about it.)

- Which careers require a person to have strong intrapersonal intelligence in order to be happy and comfortable?

◆ Have students store their definition papers in the folders they made in Lesson One.

To Simplify:

Use just the definition and symbol sheet.

To Expand:

Have students make lists of activities that call on intrapersonal intelligence. The list should be made up of things that would be hard or even impossible to do in a group.

Evaluation and Processing:

Have students consider their own experiences with intrapersonal intelligence. Are they happy working alone? Always or just sometimes? Let students discuss their conclusions if they want to.

Segment One—Lesson Eight *(cont.)*

What Is Intrapersonal Intelligence?

Definition

Intrapersonal Intelligence: It means tending to turn inward to explore one's own thoughts and feelings as part of the thinking process. It is shown through a deep awareness of inner feelings. This is the intelligence that allows people to understand themselves, their abilities, and their options. People with intrapersonal intelligence tend to be independent and self-directed and have strong opinions on controversial subjects. (Controversial subjects are subjects about which people disagree.) They have a great sense of self-confidence and enjoy working on their own projects and just being alone.

What picture or symbol could you use to remind yourself of what is meant by intrapersonal intelligence? Make a sketch of your idea in the space below.

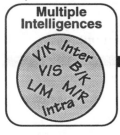

Segment One—Lesson Nine

What Are Intelligence Clusters?

Purpose: to learn about intelligence clusters and identify the ones possessed by students

Skills: knowledge, comprehension, application, analysis, synthesis, and evaluation

Intelligences: verbal/linguistic, logical/mathematical, visual/spatial, musical/rhythmic, bodily/kinesthetic, interpersonal, and/or intrapersonal

Materials:

- copies of "Using Your Symbols," one for each student
- individual folders containing definitions and symbol sketches
- large construction paper (11" x 15" or 28 cm x 38 cm), one for each student
- pieces of white drawing paper (8 ½" x 11" or 21 cm x 28 cm), one for each student
- paper, writing materials, colored pencils, etc.

Procedures:

◆ Introduce this activity by passing out the folders containing definition sheets and symbol sketches. Review the definitions. Ask students to decide, in light of what they have learned, on their own cluster of intelligences (the group of intelligences that they recognize in themselves).

◆ Ask them to look at the pictures or symbols they drew to represent the different intelligences and use the ones that represent their own intelligence cluster to create a "trademark" symbol for themselves. They can make practice sketches of this new trademark symbol on the "Using Your Symbols" page. When they are happy with their designs, have them draw them on the white drawing paper, color them, and attach the finished product to the fronts of their new folders.

◆ Store these folders away until the next group of lessons.

To Simplify:

Have an aide or parent helper work with students to facilitate this process.

To Expand:

Have students write their own definitions of the seven intelligences.

Evaluation and Processing:

Tell students that they have completed the meta-intelligences part of this study unit. They have learned to think about the intelligences. In the next activities they will be experiencing archetypal examples of each intelligence. (Ask who remembers what "archetypal" means.) Have students volunteer predictions about what these experiences will be. Write them on the board to check as you go along.

Segment One—Lesson Nine (cont.)

What Are Intelligence Clusters?

Using Your Symbols

Look at the pictures or symbols you drew to represent the different intelligences. Use the ones that represent your own intelligence cluster to create your own "trademark" in the space below.

When you are happy with your design, draw it on the white drawing paper, color it, and attach the finished product to the front of your new folder.

Segment Two—Nine Lessons

From the Middle of October Through the First Week of November

During the second segment of this minicurriculum, students will have their first experience with archetypal examples of the intelligences, beginning with the verbal/linguistic.

Verbal/linguistic intelligence means thinking and communicating through words (speaking and listening, writing and reading).

Each topic will include suggestions for exposing students to classic examples of the various genres.

The topics for this segment are listed below. A list of suggested references follows for your convenience. You may wish to look them up, check them out of the library, track down a video, and refresh your own familiarity with them. The pieces listed, in many cases, contain elements that have become a part of our culture. You should, of course, feel free to substitute or add your own favorite pieces that have made the English language come alive for you.

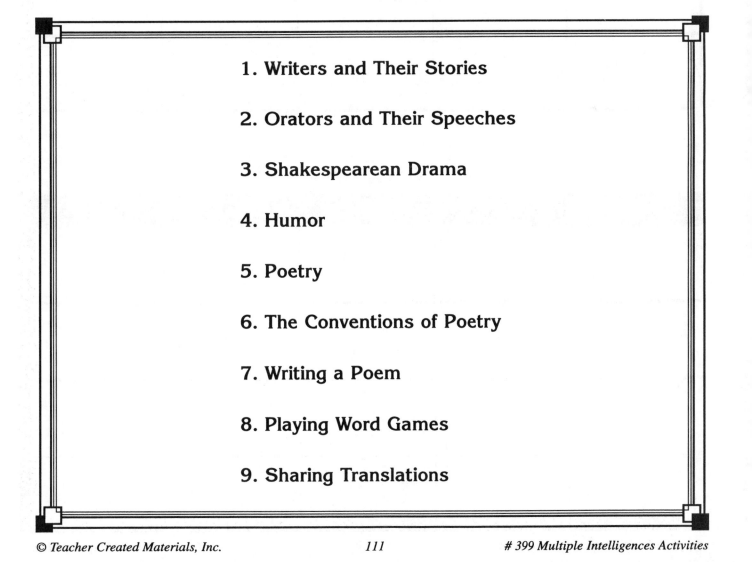

1. **Writers and Their Stories**

2. **Orators and Their Speeches**

3. **Shakespearean Drama**

4. **Humor**

5. **Poetry**

6. **The Conventions of Poetry**

7. **Writing a Poem**

8. **Playing Word Games**

9. **Sharing Translations**

Calendars for Segment Two

Directions: Use the calendars below to plan when you would like to do the nine lessons of this segment. The lessons are listed on the previous page. The highlighted weeks are the time periods which are suggested.

October

M	T	W	T	F
		S e g m e n t T w o		
		S e g m e n t T w o		

November

M	T	W	T	F
		S e g m e n t T w o		

Segment Two

References

1. Writers and Their Stories

In all of these books and stories it is important to read the originals, not modernized versions in which the language has been brought "up to date." Also, if applicable, try to find editions in which the original illustrations are reproduced.

- *Aesop's Fables*
  Aesop is thought to have been a Greek slave and storyteller who lived in the sixth century B.C. His fables were later written down by others and eventually passed along to us.

  Fables are stories in which the characters are animals who talk and act like people. All of Aesop's fables end with a moral, or lesson, based on the story.

- Carroll, Lewis: *Alice's Adventures in Wonderland* and *Through The Looking-Glass*
  Lewis Carroll was the pen name of Charles Dodgson, an English mathematician of the late eighteenth century. He is best known for his stories about Alice. In *Alice's Adventures in Wonderland,* Alice reaches Wonderland after a tumble down a rabbit hole. In *Through the Looking-Glass,* she steps through a mirror into the world on the other side. Any selection from either of these books would be enjoyable; pick your own favorite.

- Dickens, Charles: *A Tale of Two Cities*
  Charles Dickens was an English author. During the 1800s, he wrote many popular novels and stories that dealt with the problems of working class people during that time period.
  A *Tale of Two Cities* is a romantic novel set against one of the great dramatic backgrounds of history, the French Revolution. Every character and event of its complicated plot draws together into one great climax in which a man gives his life for his friends. The events at the end of the book, including Sydney Carton's speech, make a memorable, advanced reading selection.

- Kipling, Rudyard: *The Jungle Book,* and *Just So Stories*
  Rudyard Kipling, an English author of the late nineteenth and early twentieth centuries, wrote children's books such as *The Jungle Book* and *Just So Stories,* as well as novels and poems for adults.
  The *Jungle Book* is the well-known story of Mowgli, the boy who was raised by wolves. The *Just So Stories* are tales that explain things such as "How the Elephant Got Its Trunk." They are short enough to be read in their entirety.

Segment Two *(cont.)*

References *(cont.)*

1. Writers and Their Stories *(cont.)*

- Swift, Jonathan: *Gulliver's Travels*
  Jonathan Swift was an Irish author who lived in the eighteenth century. He was famous for his skill as a satirist.

Gulliver's Travels is a satire that Swift originally wrote to point out the bad things in his society, but it is also a fantasy that has great appeal for young people. Since the Lilliputians are so well known, it might be fun to select a reading from one of the other sections of the book.

2. Orators and Their Speeches

If you are not able to secure a video (or even an audio tape) of the speeches by President John F. Kennedy or Martin Luther King, Jr., you may want to read Lincoln's Gettysburg Address. The vocal quality of the other two speakers is such an integral part of their speeches that it is hard for listeners to appreciate the full quality of the speeches when they are read by others.

- Kennedy, John F.: Inaugural Address
  President John F. Kennedy was inaugurated in January of 1961 in Washington, D.C. He was the youngest person ever to be elected President. He was assassinated while in office on November 22, 1963 in Dallas, Texas.

- King, Jr., Martin Luther: "I Have A Dream . . ."
  Martin Luther King, Jr. delivered this, his most famous speech, on August 28, 1963 at a massive rally during the march on Washington in support of civil rights. He won the Nobel Peace Prize in 1964 and was assassinated in 1968.

- Lincoln, Abraham: Gettysburg Address
  Abraham Lincoln delivered this speech during the Civil War at the dedication of a military cemetery on the site of the Battle of Gettysburg. Lincoln was the sixteenth President of the United States. He was assassinated in 1865, a few days after the South surrendered.

3. Shakespearean Drama

You may want to find a recording of one or more of these selections. There are many recordings of Shakespeare's plays by famous actors and actresses. Shakespeare was a playwright and poet in late sixteenth and early seventeenth century England. He is considered to be among the greatest, if not the greatest, of English writers.

Segment Two *(cont.)*

References *(cont.)*

3. Shakespearean Drama *(cont.)*

- Shakespeare, William: *Hamlet,* "To be, or not to be: that is the question: . . ."
  These words begin Hamlet's famous soliloquy in which he considers suicide as a way out of his problems.

- Shakespeare, William: *Julius Caesar,* "Friends, Romans, Countrymen, lend me your ears . . ."
  These are the first words of a speech made by Marc Antony at Caesar's funeral.

- Shakespeare, William: *The Merchant of Venice,* "The quality of mercy is not strained . . ."
  These words begin Portia's famous speech to Shylock, a greedy moneylender, who has demanded a pound of flesh from Antonio, the title character, in payment of a debt.

4. Humor

- Henry, O.: "The Ransom of Red Chief"
  O. Henry was the pen name of William Sydney Porter, an American author of the twentieth century. He wrote short stories that often had surprise endings. Another of his well-known stories is "The Gift of the Magi."
  "The Ransom of Red Chief" is the story of a kidnapping scheme that backfired but is chiefly notable for its dry wit and appealing characterizations.

- Nash, Ogden: Any of his collected poems under various titles (One such collection is entitled *The Golden Trashery of Ogden Nashery*).
  Ogden Nash is known for his light verse, which appeared in magazines and was collected into books. His rhymes are original, and his lines are often stretched out with no concern for conventional rhythm. He has remained popular and current because his verse deals with human nature in a universal way.
  Any of Ogden Nash's poems will be fine for this experience; choose your favorites. You might want to choose a very short one like "The Baby" and one or two of the long ones.

- Thurber, James: *The Thurber Carnival* is a collection of his most famous works.
  James Thurber was a twentieth century American writer and cartoonist.
  His best-known story is "The Secret Life of Walter Mitty." One of his funniest stories is "The Night the Bed Fell on Father" from *My Life and Hard Times. Thurber's Fables for Our Times,* complete with morals, make an interesting comparison if you have already read Aesop's fables.

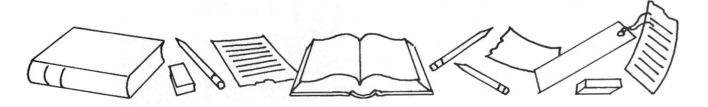

Segment Two *(cont.)*

References *(cont.)*

5. Poetry

The poems listed here usually appeal to young people who know that poetry is a way of expressing emotion through imagery.

- Aiken, Conrad: "Music I Heard"
- Clough, Arthur Hugh: "Say Not the Struggle Naught Availeth"
- Dickinson, Emily: "My Life Closed Twice"
- Frost, Robert: "The Road Not Taken"
- Hopkins, Gerard Manley: "Spring and Fall: To a Young Child"
- Rossetti, Christina: "Uphill"
- Spender, Stephen: "I Think Continually of Those" (especially the last four lines)

6. The Conventions of Poetry
- alliteration
- assonance
- blank verse
- figurative language or imagery
- foot
- free verse
- haiku
- metaphor
- meter
- personification
- rhyme
- rhyme scheme
- simile
- sonnet

7. Writing a Poem

8. Playing Word Games
- Scrabble
- crossword puzzles

9. Sharing Translations

Verbal/Linguistic

Segment Two—Lesson One

Writers and Their Stories

Purpose: to give students the first-hand experience of a story that has become a part of our cultural heritage

Skills: knowledge, comprehension, application, analysis, synthesis, and evaluation

Intelligences: verbal/linguistic, interpersonal, intrapersonal

Materials:

- a copy of the selection you have chosen to read for this lesson (Refer to the "Suggested Reference" section for ideas.)
- extra copies of the selection for students to enjoy later if they want to
- copies of "Translating the Experience," one for each student

Procedures:

- ◆ Have students review the definition of verbal/linguistic intelligence.
- ◆ Introduce this experience by giving students the title of the lesson and the title and author of the piece you have selected. (If you wish, you can also give them a brief biographical sketch of the author.)
- ◆ Read the selection aloud to the class. (If you have chosen one of Aesop's fables or one of Kipling's stories, you will be able to read the whole piece. If you have chosen a longer work, pre-select a meaningful passage that captures the spirit of the work. (For a brief synopsis, see the "References" section.)
- ◆ Without any discussion, ask students to follow the directions on the sheet entitled "Translating the Experience."
- ◆ Use these sheets for discussion during Evaluation and Processing and then place them in the students' folders from Segment One.

To Simplify:

Omit "Translating the Experience."

To Expand:

Ask students to find and read something else by the same author.

Evaluation and Processing:

Allow students to share and discuss their "Translating the Experience" sheets.

Segment Two—Lesson One *(cont.)*

Writers and Their Stories

Translating the Experience

Think about the experience you just had. It was a verbal/linguistic experience: your teacher read something that was written, and the words were spoken aloud so you could listen to them.

Think about your reaction to the experience. Do not express your reaction in words! Instead, decide how you could translate your reaction by expressing it through another one of the seven intelligences.

Which intelligence will you use to translate your experience?

_____

What materials, if any, will you need?

_____   _____

_____   _____

_____   _____

Will you need time to prepare your translation? How much?

_____

How will you share your translation with the class?

_____

_____

_____

_____

_____

_____

_____

Verbal/Linguistic

Segment Two—Lesson Two

Orators and Their Speeches

Purpose: to give students the first-hand experience of a speech that has become a part of our cultural heritage

Skills: knowledge, comprehension, application, analysis, synthesis, and evaluation

Intelligences: verbal/linguistic, interpersonal, intrapersonal

Materials:

- a copy of the selection you have chosen to read for this lesson or a video or audio tape of the speech (See the "References" section for selection suggestions.)
- extra copies of the selection for students to enjoy later if they want to
- copies of "Translating the Experience," one for each student

Procedures:

◆ Have students review the definition of verbal/linguistic intelligence.

◆ Introduce this experience by giving students the title of the lesson and the name of the orator of the speech and the occasion for which it was delivered. (If you wish, you can also give them a brief biographical sketch of the orator.)

◆ Read the selection aloud or play the video or audio tape for the class.

◆ Without any discussion, ask students to follow the directions on the sheet entitled "Translating the Experience."

◆ Use these sheets for discussion during Evaluation and Processing and then place them in the students' folders from Segment One.

To Simplify:

Omit "Translating the Experience."

To Expand:

Ask students to find out if the orator was famous for any other speeches. What? When? Where? etc.

Evaluation and Processing:

Allow students to share and discuss their "Translating the Experience" sheets.

Segment Two—Lesson Two *(cont.)*

Orators and Their Speeches

Translating the Experience

Think about the experience you just had. It was a verbal/linguistic experience: you either heard your teacher read something that was written, speaking the words aloud so you could listen to them, or you saw and heard a video or heard a recording of the person who actually made the speech.

Think about your reaction to the experience. Do not express your reaction in words! Instead, decide how you could translate your reaction by expressing it through another one of the seven intelligences.

Which intelligence will you use to translate your experience?

_____

What materials, if any, will you need?

_____   _____

_____   _____

_____   _____

Will you need time to prepare your translation? How much?

_____

How will you share your translation with the class?

_____

_____

_____

_____

_____

_____

_____

Verbal/Linguistic

Segment Two—Lesson Three

Shakespearean Drama

Purpose: to give students the first-hand experience of a speech from a play that has become a part of our cultural heritage

Skills: knowledge, comprehension, application, analysis, synthesis, and evaluation

Intelligences: verbal/linguistic, interpersonal, intrapersonal

Materials:

- a copy of the selection or selections you have chosen to read for this lesson or a video or audio tape of the selection (For selection suggestions see the "References" section.)
- extra copies of the selection for students to enjoy later if they want to
- copies of "Translating the Experience," one for each student

Procedures:

- ◆ Have students review the definition of verbal/linguistic intelligence.
- ◆ Introduce this experience by giving students the title of the play, the name of the character who is making the speech, and the occasion on which the speech was delivered. (If you wish, you can also give them a brief biographical sketch of William Shakespeare.)
- ◆ Read the selection aloud or play the video or audio tape for the class. (You will probably be able to obtain a recording of these selections from a library. Most of the famous Shakespearean actors have recorded their performances.)
- ◆ Without any discussion, ask students to follow the directions on the sheet entitled "Translating the Experience."
- ◆ Use these sheets for discussion during Evaluation and Processing and then place them in the students' folders from Segment One.

To Simplify:

Omit "Translating the Experience."

To Expand:

Ask students to find other famous speeches from other famous plays, both by Shakespeare and other dramatists, and note this information: author, title, character, first line of the speech.

Evaluation and Processing:

Allow students to share and discuss their "Translating the Experience" sheets.

Segment Two—Lesson Three *(cont.)*

Shakespearean Drama

Translating the Experience

Think about the experience you just had. It was a verbal/linguistic experience: you either heard your teacher read something that was written, speaking the words aloud so you could listen to them, or you saw and heard a video, or heard a recording, of an actor playing the part of a character in a play.

Think about your reaction to the experience. Do not express your reaction in words! Instead, decide how you could translate your reaction by expressing it through another one of the seven intelligences.

Which intelligence will you use to translate your experience?

_____

What materials, if any, will you need?

_____   _____

_____   _____

_____   _____

Will you need time to prepare your translation? How much?

_____

How will you share your translation with the class?

_____

_____

_____

_____

_____

_____

_____

Verbal/Linguistic

Segment Two—Lesson Four

Humor

Purpose: to give students a first-hand experience with humorous writing

Skills: knowledge, comprehension, application, analysis, synthesis, and evaluation

Intelligences: verbal/linguistic, interpersonal, intrapersonal

Materials:

- a copy of the selection or selections you have chosen to read for this lesson (See the "References" section for selection ideas.)
- extra copies of the selection for students to enjoy later if they want to
- copies of "Translating the Experience," one for each student

Procedures:

- ◆ Have students review the definition of verbal/linguistic intelligence.
- ◆ Introduce this experience by giving students the title of the lesson and the title and author of the piece you have selected. (If you wish, you can also give them a brief biographical sketch of the author.)
- ◆ Read the selection aloud to the class. (If you have chosen "The Ransom of Red Chief," you will probably want to read the whole story. You can read a number of Ogden Nash's verses and probably more than one of Thurber's stories, depending on your choice(s). For brief descriptions of your options, see the "Suggested References" section.)
- ◆ Without any discussion, ask students to follow the directions on the sheet entitled "Translating the Experience."
- ◆ Use these sheets for discussion during Evaluation and Processing and then place them in the students' folders from Segment One.

To Simplify:

Omit "Translating the Experience."

To Expand:

Ask students to find other examples of humorous writing to share with the class. Ask them to note this information: author, title, and a brief synopsis.

Evaluation and Processing:

Allow students to share and discuss their "Translating the Experience" sheets.

Segment Two—Lesson Four *(cont.)*

Humor

Translating the Experience

Think about the experience you just had. It was a verbal/linguistic experience: your teacher read something that was written, and the words were spoken aloud so that you could listen to them.

Think about your reaction to the experience. How did your reaction differ from your reaction to oratory or Shakespearean drama? Do not express your reaction in words! Instead, decide how you could translate your reaction by expressing it through another one of the intelligences.

Which intelligence will you use to translate your experience?

_____

What materials, if any, will you need?

_____   _____

_____   _____

_____   _____

Will you need time to prepare your translation? How much?

_____

How will you share your translation with the class?

_____

_____

_____

_____

_____

_____

_____

Verbal/Linguistic

Segment Two—Lesson Five

Poetry

Purpose: to give students the first-hand experience of lyric poetry

Skills: knowledge, comprehension, application, analysis, synthesis, and evaluation

Intelligences: verbal/linguistic, interpersonal, intrapersonal

Materials:

- a copy of the selection or selections you have chosen to read for this lesson (See the "References" section for selection ideas.)
- copies of the selections for students to read along with you, as well as to enjoy later (Save these for use in the next lesson.)
- copies of "Translating or Not Translating the Experience," both pages, one set for each student (Note: Take a moment to look over these activity sheets before you make the copies. You may wish to ask your students ahead of time if they are more interested in the subject matter of the first or second page. This way you can make the correct number of copies and not waste paper.)

Procedures:

- ◆ Have students review the definition of verbal/linguistic intelligence.
- ◆ Introduce this experience by giving students the title of the lesson and the titles and authors of the poems you have selected. (See the "Suggested References" section.)
- ◆ Pass out copies of the selections for the students to use as you read the selections aloud to the class. (The poems listed make a nice range of experience. Since they are short, you may want to include all of them.)
- ◆ Without any discussion, ask students to follow the directions on the two sheets entitled "Translating or Not Translating the Experience."
- ◆ Use these sheets for discussion during Evaluation and Processing and then place them in the students' folders from Segment One.

To Simplify:

Omit "Translating or Not Translating the Experience."

To Expand:

Ask students to find other examples of poetry that they would like to share with the class. Ask them to note this information: author, title, and the type of poetry.

Evaluation and Processing:

Allow students to share and discuss their "Translating or Not Translating the Experience" sheets.

Segment Two—Lesson Five *(cont.)*

Poetry

Translating or Not Translating the Experience

Think about the experience you just had. It was a verbal/linguistic experience: your teacher read something that was written, and the words were read aloud so that you could listen to them.

Think about your reaction to the experience. This time you will have two options: You can decide how you could translate your reaction by expressing it through another one of the intelligences, or you can stay within the verbal/linguistic intelligence and write about your reaction to one or more pieces of the poetry.

(If you choose to stay within the verbal/linguistic intelligence, go on to the next page.)

If you choose to translate your experience, which intelligence will you use? _____

What materials, if any, will you need?

_____   _____

_____   _____

_____   _____

Will you need time to prepare your translation? How much?

_____

How will you share your translation with the class?

_____

_____

_____

_____

_____

_____

_____

Segment Two—Lesson Five *(cont.)*

Poetry

Translating or Not Translating the Experience *(cont.)*

You have chosen to stay within the verbal/linguistic intelligence and write about one or more pieces of the poetry you have heard. Look at your copy of the poetry and try to answer the following questions.

Which poem did you like best?_____

_____

Why did you like it best? Was it the idea, the emotion, the language, or something else? _____

_____

_____

_____

What does the poem actually say? Summarize its idea in prose.

_____

_____

_____

_____

Is the poem's message more effective in prose or in the original poetic form? Why?_____

_____

_____

_____

_____

_____

Verbal/Linguistic

Segment Two—Lesson Six

The Conventions of Poetry

Purpose: to give students the tools with which to write poetry of different kinds

Skills: knowledge, comprehension, application, analysis, synthesis, and evaluation

Intelligences: verbal/linguistic, interpersonal, intrapersonal

Materials:

- copies of "Definitions and Examples," one for each student
- a copy of the selection or selections you chose to read for the previous lesson
- copies of the poetry selections from the previous lesson
- copies of "Using the Information," one for each student

Procedures:

◆ Have students review the definition of verbal/linguistic intelligence.

◆ Pass out copies of "Definitions and Examples."

◆ Pass out copies of the poetry selections from the previous lesson. Pass out copies of "Using the Information." You may have students work on them individually (intrapersonal) or in groups (interpersonal).

◆ Use these sheets for discussion during Evaluation and Processing and then place them in the students' folders from Segment One.

To Simplify:

Omit one or more parts of "Using the Information."

To Expand:

Ask students to find examples of poetry that meet the definitions of these terms: free verse, blank verse, haiku, and sonnet. Ask them to note the author and title of each example.

Evaluation and Processing:

Allow students to share and discuss their "Using the Information" sheets.

Segment Two—Lesson Six *(cont.)*

The Conventions of Poetry

Definition and Example Dictionary

alliteration: the repetition of consonants, especially initial consonants. (For example, "The trees tossed their branches as we tramped through the windy town.")

assonance: the repetition of vowel sounds in two or more words, for example, reach and stream

blank verse: unrhymed iambic (one unaccented and one unaccented syllable) pentameter (five feet) (For example, "The qua li ty of mer cy is not strained.")

figurative language or imagery: language that appeals to any of the senses

foot: a unit of meter consisting of one accented and one or more unaccented syllables. (⌣╱ is an iambic foot.) All of the different feet (combinations of syllables) have special names.

free verse: verse that does not conform to any fixed pattern of rhyme or meter

haiku: an unrhymed Japanese verse form consisting of three lines of 5, 7, and 5 syllables, respectively

metaphor: an implied comparison without the use of <u>like</u> or <u>as</u> (For example, The <u>wind was a roaring lion.</u>)

meter: the organized rhythm of a line of poetry determined by the relationship between the accented and unaccented syllables of words

personification: things or abstract qualities treated as if they were real persons

rhyme: correspondence of sound between stressed syllables at the ends of words or lines of verse (The spelling *rime* is preferred by many as historically correct.)

rhyme scheme: the pattern of end rhymes used in a poem, usually indicated by letters (A stanza in which the first and third lines and the second and fourth lines rhyme would be indicated as abab. A stanza in which only the second and fourth lines rhyme would be indicated as abcb.)

simile: a statement of comparison using *like* or *as*; For example, the wind was like a roaring lion.

sonnet: an iambic pentameter poem of fourteen lines—major forms are Italian and English.

Segment Two—Lesson Six *(cont.)*

The Conventions of Poetry

Using the Information

Do any of the poems contain figurative language? Write an example of figurative language. Include the author and the title of the poem.

_____

_____

_____

_____

_____

What is the rhyme scheme of "Uphill" by Christina Rossetti?

_____

Do any of the poems contain alliteration? Write the name of the poem and an example of the alliteration it contains.

_____

_____

_____

Find a simile or a metaphor in one of the poems. Write it, the title, and the author of the poem.

_____

_____

_____

_____

_____

_____

Verbal/Linguistic

Segment Two—Lesson Seven

Writing a Poem

Purpose: to give students the opportunity to create an original poem

Skills: knowledge, comprehension, application, analysis, synthesis, and evaluation

Intelligences: verbal/linguistic, interpersonal, intrapersonal

Materials:

- copies of "Writing a Poem," one for each student
- writing materials

Procedures:

◆ Have students review the definition of verbal/linguistic intelligence.

◆ Pass out copies of "Writing a Poem."

◆ Tell students that they may use "Definitions and Examples" from the previous lesson.

◆ Original poems may be shared and discussed during Evaluation and Processing and then placed in the student folders from Segment One.

To Simplify:

Allow students to work with a partner or with an aide or helper, if they wish.

To Expand:

Have students illustrate their completed poems.

Evaluation and Processing:

Share and discuss original poems. Was it enjoyable? Was it hard? Would they continue to write poetry occasionally on their own?

Segment Two—Lesson Seven *(cont.)*

Writing a Poem

Use your experience with poetry and all of the information you have gathered to write a poem of your own. You may use any form, rhymed or unrhymed. Try to include some figurative language.

_____

_____

_____

_____

_____

_____

_____

_____

_____

_____

_____

_____

_____

_____

_____

_____

_____

_____

_____

_____

Verbal/Linguistic

Segment Two—Lesson Eight

Playing Word Games

Purpose: to give students the opportunity to play games associated with verbal/linguistic intelligence

Skills: knowledge, comprehension, application, analysis, synthesis, and evaluation

Intelligences: verbal/linguistic, interpersonal, intrapersonal

Materials:

- a number of word/vocabulary games
- crossword puzzles of varying levels of difficulty
- copies of "Evaluating the Activity," one for each student
- writing materials

Procedures:

- ◆ Have students review the definition of verbal/linguistic intelligence.
- ◆ Ask them to choose an activity and begin.

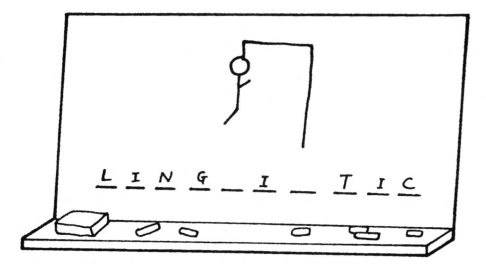

- ◆ Allow time for students to complete an evaluation at the end of the activity.
- ◆ Place the evaluation sheets into the students' folders.

To Simplify:

Allow students to work with an aide or helper, if they wish.

To Expand:

Keep games and puzzles on hand for use during activity times.

Evaluation and Processing:

Share and discuss evaluation sheets.

Segment Two—Lesson Eight *(cont.)*

Playing Word Games

Evaluate the activity on page 133 by responding to the following questions.

1. Which game did you play? _____

_____

2. If you were playing with a group, will you continue the game later? _____

_____

3. If you were working alone, will you finish later?_____

_____

4. Would you ever play this game outside of school? Where? When? _____

_____

_____

_____

_____

_____

5. Is there another type of game that you prefer? What is it? _____

_____

_____

_____

_____

_____

_____

Rate this activity from 1 to 10, with10 being best (circle choice):

| 1 | 2 | 3 | 4 | 5 | 6 | 7 | 8 | 9 | 10 |

Verbal/Linguistic

Segment Two—Lesson Nine

Sharing Translations

Purpose: to give students the opportunity to share their various translations and activity sheets from this segment

Skills: knowledge, comprehension, application, analysis, synthesis, and evaluation

Intelligences: Potentially, all may be involved

Materials:

- individual student folders

Procedures:

◆ Invite students to share their translations and activity sheets from this segment.

◆ Allow time for presentations and positive acknowledgements of effort.

To Simplify:

Allow students to work with an aide or helper, if they wish.

To Expand:

Encourage students to use the techniques they learned in this segment on future assignments.

Evaluation and Processing:

This activity is actually an evaluation and processing of the entire segment.

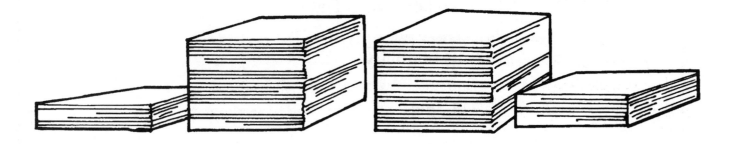

Segment Three—Nine Lessons

From the Middle of November Through the
First Week of December

During the third segment of this minicurriculum, students will have their second experience with archetypal examples of the intelligences, as we consider the logical/mathematical.

Logical/mathematical intelligence means thinking and communicating like a scientist: organizing and using data, looking at patterns and relationships, solving problems, and playing strategy games.

Each topic will include an activity based on current logical and mathematical thinking.

The topics selected for this segment are listed below. Brief descriptions and/or explanations follow for your convenience. You may wish to refresh your own familiarity with these areas. You should, of course, feel free to substitute or add your own favorite topics. If this is "your" intelligence, you will have favorite topics that make this area come alive for you.

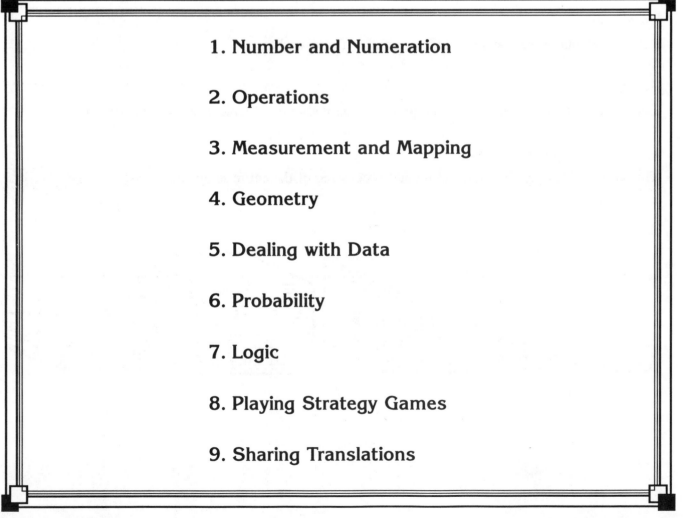

1. Number and Numeration

2. Operations

3. Measurement and Mapping

4. Geometry

5. Dealing with Data

6. Probability

7. Logic

8. Playing Strategy Games

9. Sharing Translations

Calendars for Segment Three

Directions: Use the calendars below to plan when you would like to do the nine lessons of this segment. The lessons are listed on the previous page. The highlighted weeks are the time periods which are suggested.

November

M	T	W	T	F
		Segment Three		
		Segment Three		

December

M	T	W	T	F
		Segment Three		

Segment Three

References

1. Number and Numeration

Numbers can be used to . . .

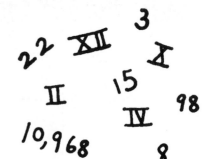

- show quantities (how many) of both whole objects and parts of wholes
- stand for very large and very small quantities through the use of grouping and place value
- represent quantity in many ways, including equivalence
- make comparisons and identify locations

2. Operations

Understanding operations includes . . .

- knowing what actions are represented by the operations
- knowing how these actions relate to one another
- knowing what operations are appropriate in individual situations
- knowing what tools will be most useful in finding the answers—mental arithmetic, paper and pencil, or a calculator

3. Measurement and Mapping

Measurement involves . . .

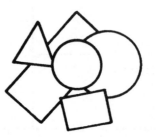

- selecting an appropriate unit, standard or nonstandard
- comparing that unit with the object being measured and determining the number of units

Mapping involves measurement in determining . . .
- length
- area
- distance

4. Geometry

Measuring geometric figures includes finding . . .

- surface area
- perimeter or circumference
- volume

Segment Three *(cont.)*

References *(cont.)*

4. Geometry *(cont.)*

Visualizing and representing shapes involves . . .

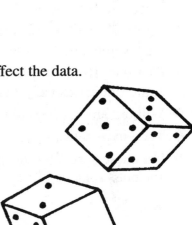

- symmetry
- rotation
- reflection
- perspective
- drawing three-dimensional shapes on paper

5. Dealing with Data

The process of dealing with data includes these concepts:

- Data can reflect information drawn from the real world.
- In collecting information, the way questions are asked can affect the data.
- There is a variety of ways to organize and present data.
- A sample can be used to represent a whole group.

6. Probability

The study of probability at this level involves . . .

- informal observations of chance
- recording data and reporting results

7. Logic

Logic in elementary and middle school can be interpreted broadly to include the following skills:

- understanding patterns and the ability to continue them
- sorting and classifying by attributes, similarities, and differences
- making generalizations from collected data

8. Playing Strategy Games

Strategy games include . . .

- checkers
- chess

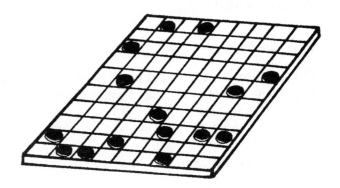

9. Sharing Translations

**Logical/
Mathematical**

Segment Three—Lesson One

Number and Numeration

Purpose: to give students the first-hand experience of using different systems of numeration

Skills: knowledge, comprehension, application, analysis, synthesis, and evaluation

Intelligences: logical/mathematical, verbal/linguistic, interpersonal, intrapersonal

Materials:

- copies of "Different Numerals for Numbers," one for each student
- copies of "Translating the Experience," one for each student

Procedures:

◆ Have students review the definition of logical/mathematical intelligence.

◆ Introduce this experience by discussing the difference between "number" and "numeration."(See the "References" section.)

◆ Pass out "Different Numerals for Numbers." Students may work in groups (interpersonal) or alone (intrapersonal); it is up to you.

◆ Without any further discussion, ask students to follow the directions on the activity sheet.

◆ Then have students work individually on the sheet entitled "Translating the Experience."

◆ Use these sheets for discussion during Evaluation and Processing and then place them in the students' folders.

To Simplify:

Omit "Translating the Experience."

To Expand:

Ask students to find out about another system of numeration, or about the history of one of the numeration systems, and make a report to the class.

Evaluation and Processing:

Allow students to share and discuss their "Translating the Experience" sheets.

Note:

The two things our system has that the Roman system lacked are place value and the concept of zero. This is the answer to the second problem on "Translating the Experience."

Segment Three—Lesson One *(cont.)*

Number and Numeration

Different Numerals for Numbers

The numerals we use are called Arabic numerals because they were originally brought to Europe by the Arabs. They look like this: 0, 1, 2, 3, 4, 5, 6, 7, 8, 9.

The numerals used by the ancient Romans, called Roman numerals, look like some of the capital letters in our alphabet. Here are some of them:

I = 1	XI = 11	C = 100
II = 2	XII = 12	CCC = 300
III = 3	XIII = 13	CD = 400
IV = 4	XIV = 14	D = 500
V = 5	XV = 15	DC = 600
VI = 6	XX = 20	CM = 900
VII = 7	XL = 40	M = 1000
VIII = 8	L = 50	MC = 1100
IX = 9	LX = 60	
X = 10	XC = 90	

Study the relationship between these two numeral systems and figure out the answers below.

17 = _____	28 = _____	55 = _____
64 = _____	99 = _____	101 = _____
222 = _____	624 = _____	47 = _____
1025 = _____	492 = _____	1995 = _____
XVII = _____	XXVIII = _____	LXIV = _____
LV = _____	CI = _____	XCIX = _____
MCMXCV = _____	MCDXCII = _____	MXXV = _____
DCXXIV = _____	CCXXII = _____	CMXLVII = _____

What did you discover about these two sets of answers?

_____

_____

_____

Segment Three—Lesson One *(cont.)*

Number and Numeration

Translating the Experience

Think about the experience you just had. It was a logical/mathematical experience. You were thinking about numbers, the numerals that stand for them, and their relationships.

Think about your reaction to the experience. In this part of learning about the multiple intelligences you will be translating logical/mathematical experiences by explaining them in written words. Many people feel that logical/mathematical thinking can be made clear by writing about it.

How did you start to figure out the problems? What did you do next? Did you make any false starts? If so, how did you go about figuring out what to do next?

_____

_____

_____

_____

_____

_____

There are two important differences between the way we write numbers in Arabic numerals and the way the Romans wrote numbers. Our system has two things that they did not have. Did you discover what they are? Write about them below.

_____

_____

_____

_____

_____

_____

_____

Logical/Mathematical

Segment Three—Lesson Two

Operations

Purpose: to give students the experience of finding appropriate ways to determine whether or not their computed answers fall within a reasonable range

Skills: knowledge, comprehension, application, analysis, synthesis, and evaluation

Intelligences: logical/mathematical, verbal/linguistic, interpersonal, intrapersonal

Materials:

- copies of "Reasonable Answers," one for each student
- copies of "Translating the Experience," one for each student

Procedures:

◆ Have students review the definition of logical/mathematical intelligence.

◆ Introduce this experience by discussing the tools that can be used to find answers and the relationships among them. (See the "References" section.)

◆ Pass out "Reasonable Answers." Students may work in groups (interpersonal) or alone (intrapersonal).

◆ Without any further discussion, ask students to follow the directions on the sheet entitled "Reasonable Answers."

◆ Then have students work individually on the sheet entitled "Translating the Experience."

◆ Use these sheets for discussion during Evaluation and Processing and then place them in the students' folders.

To Simplify:

Omit "Translating the Experience."

To Expand:

Have students experiment with different functions on their calculators. See if they can figure out how to do problems with multiple steps. Each person who learns something new can explain it to someone else.

Evaluation and Processing:

Allow students to share and discuss their "Translating the Experience" sheets.

Note:

The additional steps needed for the second problem in "Translating the Experience" would probably be rounding and estimating.

Segment Three—Lesson Two *(cont.)*

Operations

Reasonable Answers

The four basic operations in arithmetic are:

_____ _____ _____ _____

Suppose you were using a calculator to multiply 800 x 600. The answer you would get is 1400.

Is this a reasonable answer? _____

How do you know? _____

_____

How can you check it? Can you think of more than one way?

_____

_____

_____

Suppose you were using a calculator to multiply 789 x 591. The answer you would get is 1380.

Is this a reasonable answer? _____

How do you know? _____

_____

How can you check it? Can you think of more than one way? _____

_____

_____

_____

_____

Segment Three—Lesson Two *(cont.)*

Operations

Translating the Experience

Think about the experience you just had. It was a logical/mathematical experience. You were considering operations and their given answers and were asked whether or not these answers were in a reasonable range.

Think about your reaction to the experience. In this part of learning about the multiple intelligences you will be translating logical/mathematical experiences by explaining them in written words. Many people feel that logical/mathematical thinking can be made clear by writing about it.

How did you start to figure out the problems? What did you do next? Did you make any false starts? If so, how did you go about figuring out what to do then?

_____

_____

_____

_____

_____

_____

Are these problems similar? Were there any steps you took in solving the second problem that you did not take in solving the first one? What were they? Explain what you did. _____

_____

_____

_____

_____

Segment Three—Lesson Three

Measurement and Mapping

Purpose: to give students the experience of applying measurement skills to map reading

Skills: knowledge, comprehension, application, analysis, synthesis, and evaluation

Intelligences: logical/mathematical, verbal/linguistic, interpersonal, intrapersonal

Materials:

- copies of "How Far Is It?", one for each student
- an atlas for each group or individual student
- copies of "Translating the Experience," one for each student

Procedures:

◆ Have students review the definition of logical/mathematical intelligence.

◆ Introduce this experience with a quick, general review of measurement. (See the "References" section.)

◆ Continue by reminding students to look at the "scales" that appear on maps.

◆ Pass out "How Far Is It?" Students may work in groups (interpersonal) or alone (intrapersonal); it is up to you. You may prefer group work in this case because of the need for atlases.

◆ Without any further discussion, ask students to follow the directions on the sheet entitled "How Far Is It?"

◆ Then have students work individually on the sheet entitled "Translating the Experience."

◆ Use these sheets for discussion during Evaluation and Processing and then place them in the students' folders.

To Simplify:

Omit "Translating the Experience."

To Expand:

Have students continue to find out how far it is from one place of their choice to another. Encourage them to share their information and check results with others.

Evaluation and Processing:

Allow students to share and discuss their "Translating the Experience" sheets.

Segment Three—Lesson Three (cont.)

Measurement and Mapping

How Far Is It?

Open your atlas and choose a map that shows at least three different countries in South America.

Using the scale on the map, find out how far apart these places are in miles. Use the measuring tool that seems appropriate to you.

1. Find the distance between the capital of the country and the city that is farthest north.

   Name of the country _____

   Name of the capital city _____

   Name of the city farthest north _____

   Distance apart in miles _____

2. Find the distance between the capital of a second country and its city that is farthest south.

   Name of the country _____

   Name of the capital city _____

   Name of the city farthest south _____

   Distance apart in miles _____

3. Find the distance between the capital of a third country and its city that is farthest east or west.

   Name of the country _____

   Name of the capital city _____

   Name of the city farthest east or west _____

   Distance apart in miles _____

Segment Three—Lesson Three *(cont.)*

Measurement and Mapping

Translating the Experience

Think about the experience you just had. It was a logical/mathematical experience. You were using measurement skills to determine distance on a map.

Think about your reaction to the experience. In this part of learning about the multiple intelligences you will be translating logical/mathematical experiences by explaining them in written words. Many people feel that logical/mathematical thinking can be made clear by writing about it.

How did you start to figure out the problems? What did you do next? Did you make any false starts? If so, how did you go about figuring out what to do next?

_____

_____

_____

_____

Did you use a standard or nonstandard measuring tool? Why?

_____

_____

_____

How did you know which city was the capital city?

_____

_____

_____

_____

Logical/
Mathematical

Segment Three—Lesson Four

Geometry

Purpose: to give students the experience of working with a Mobius strip

Skills: knowledge, comprehension, application, analysis, synthesis, and evaluation

Intelligences: logical/mathematical, verbal/linguistic, visual/spatial, interpersonal, intrapersonal

Materials:

- copies of "The Mobius Strip," both pages, for each student
- strips of paper about two inches (5 cm) wide and two feet (61 cm) long, one for each student, plus extras (These can be cut from a roll of white shelf paper.)
- tape
- copies of "Translating the Experience," one for each student

Procedures:

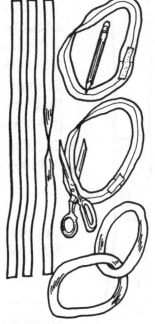

- ◆ Have students review the definition of logical/mathematical intelligence.
- ◆ Introduce this experience with a quick overview of geometry. (See the "References" section.)
- ◆ Tell students that the investigation they will be conducting really belongs to a branch of mathematics called topology. It is like regular geometry because it deals with points, lines, and surfaces, but there are interesting differences.
- ◆ Pass out both pages of "The Mobius Strip." Students may work in groups (interpersonal) or alone (intrapersonal).
- ◆ Without any further discussion, ask students to follow the directions on "The Mobius Strip" pages.
- ◆ Then have students work individually on the sheet entitled "Translating the Experience."
- ◆ Use these sheets for discussion during Evaluation and Processing and then place them in the students' folders.

To Simplify:

Omit "Translating the Experience."

To Expand:

Have students find out more about topology and share their information with the class.

Evaluation and Processing:

Allow students to share and discuss their "Translating the Experience" sheets as well as their completed charts from the second page of "The Mobius Strip."

Segment Three—Lesson Four *(cont.)*

Geometry

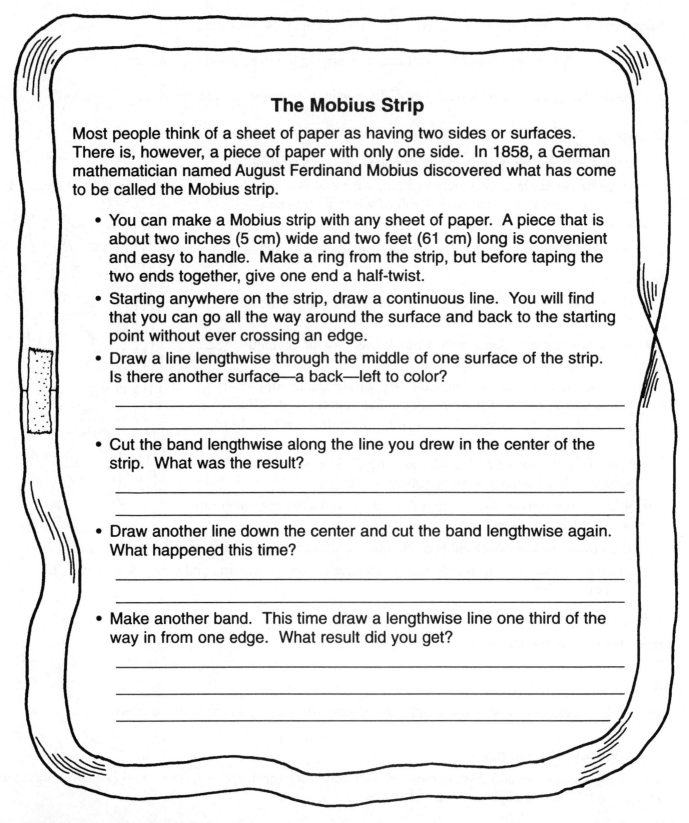

The Mobius Strip

Most people think of a sheet of paper as having two sides or surfaces. There is, however, a piece of paper with only one side. In 1858, a German mathematician named August Ferdinand Mobius discovered what has come to be called the Mobius strip.

- You can make a Mobius strip with any sheet of paper. A piece that is about two inches (5 cm) wide and two feet (61 cm) long is convenient and easy to handle. Make a ring from the strip, but before taping the two ends together, give one end a half-twist.

- Starting anywhere on the strip, draw a continuous line. You will find that you can go all the way around the surface and back to the starting point without ever crossing an edge.

- Draw a line lengthwise through the middle of one surface of the strip. Is there another surface—a back—left to color?

  _____

  _____

- Cut the band lengthwise along the line you drew in the center of the strip. What was the result?

  _____

  _____

- Draw another line down the center and cut the band lengthwise again. What happened this time?

  _____

  _____

- Make another band. This time draw a lengthwise line one third of the way in from one edge. What result did you get?

  _____

  _____

  _____

Segment Three—Lesson Four (cont.)

Geometry

The Mobius Strip (cont.)

Complete the chart below to discover what happens when you change the number of twists and the way you cut the strip. Later, you can compare results with your classmates.

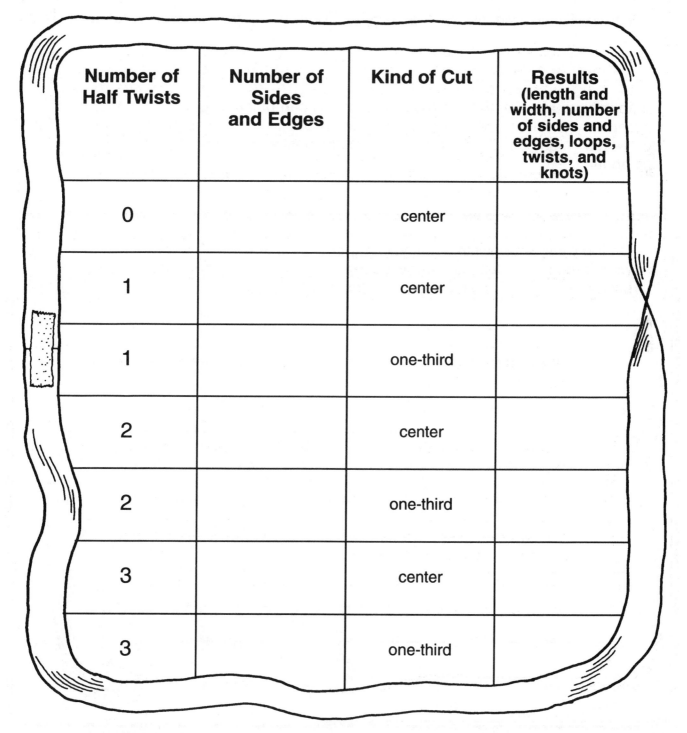

Number of Half Twists	Number of Sides and Edges	Kind of Cut	Results (length and width, number of sides and edges, loops, twists, and knots)
0		center	
1		center	
1		one-third	
2		center	
2		one-third	
3		center	
3		one-third	

Segment Three—Lesson Four *(cont.)*

Geometry

Translating the Experience

Think about the experience you just had. It was a logical/mathematical experience. You were investigating the characteristics of the Mobius strip.

If you tried to visualize what was happening, you were using another intelligence too. Which one?

_____

Think about your reaction to the experience. In this part of learning about the multiple intelligences, you will be translating logical/mathematical experiences by explaining them in written words. Many people feel that logical/mathematical thinking can be made clear by writing about it.

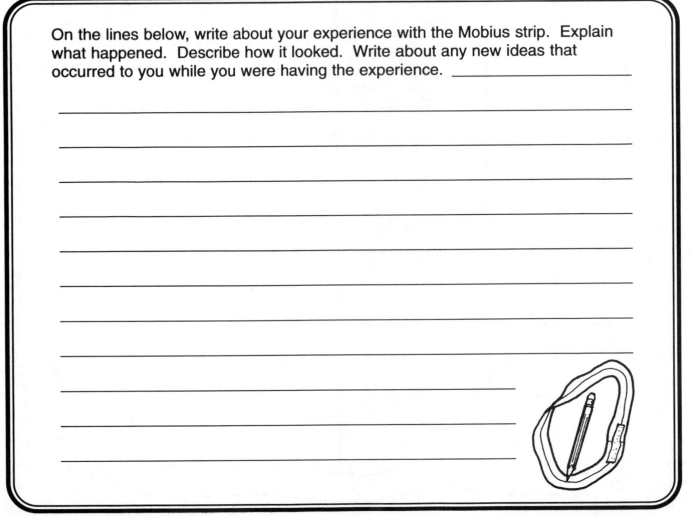

On the lines below, write about your experience with the Mobius strip. Explain what happened. Describe how it looked. Write about any new ideas that occurred to you while you were having the experience. _____

_____

_____

_____

_____

_____

_____

_____

_____

_____

Segment Three—Lesson Five

Dealing With Data

Purpose: to give students the experience of choosing a representative sample from an entire group or population

Skills: knowledge, comprehension, application, analysis, synthesis, and evaluation

Intelligences: logical/mathematical, verbal/linguistic, interpersonal, intrapersonal

Materials:

- copies of "A Representative Sample," both pages for each student
- 50 black marbles and 100 red marbles per group
- bags or boxes to put the marbles in
- copies of "Translating the Experience," one for each student

Procedures:

- ◆ Have students review the definition of logical/mathematical intelligence.
- ◆ Introduce this experience with a quick overview of dealing with data (statistics). (See the "References" section.)
- ◆ Call your students' attention to the fact that surveys almost never reflect an entire population. Instead, a sample is taken, and the results of the sample are used as if they reflected the whole group from which they were taken. The question is: How big a sample is necessary to reliably represent the population as a whole?
- ◆ Pass out both pages of "A Representative Sample." You will probably want students to work in groups (interpersonal) for this activity because of the materials that are required. However, if you have students who are comfortable only when working alone (intrapersonal), they could take turns in using the materials.
- ◆ Without any further discussion, ask students to follow the directions on "A Representative Sample."
- ◆ Then have students work individually on the sheet entitled "Translating the Experience."
- ◆ Use these sheets for discussion during Evaluation and Processing and then place them in the students' folders.

To Simplify:

Omit "Translating the Experience."

To Expand:

Have students look at current magazines and newspapers to find articles based on surveys.

Evaluation and Processing:

Allow students to share and discuss their "Translating the Experience" sheets, as well as the "A Representative Sample" pages.

Segment Three—Lesson Five *(cont.)*

Dealing With Data

A Representative Sample

In this activity you will determine how large a sample should be in order to accurately represent a whole population.

1. Count the marbles in your bag or box. Record this information:

   Total number of marbles:_____

   Number of black marbles: _____

   Number of red marbles:_____

2. Make a generalization.

   There are _____ black for every _____ red.

   or

   There are _____ red for every _____ black.

3. Begin sampling. When you find a sample that matches your generalization, repeat it to verify your results.

4. Decide on the size of your first sample: _____ marbles

   Without looking, count out your marble sample.

   The first sample contained _____ black and _____ red.

   This **did / did not** match the generalization for the entire population. (*Circle one.*)

   If the results did not match the generalization, choose another sample size and try again. If the results did match, drop down to #8.

5. Decide on the size of your second sample: _____ marbles

   Without looking, count out your marble sample.

   The second sample contained _____ black and _____ red.

   This **did / did not** match the generalization for the entire population. (*Circle one.*)

   If the results did not match the generalization, choose another sample size and try again. If the results did match, drop down to #8.

Segment Three—Lesson Five *(cont.)*

Dealing With Data

A Representative Sample *(cont.)*

6. Decide on the size of your third sample: _____ marbles

   Without looking, count out your marble sample.

   The third sample contained _____ black and _____ red.

   This **did / did not** match the generalization for the entire population. *(Circle one.)*

7. If you did not find the needed results in the first three samples, continue sampling until you are satisfied with your results. Record these additional results on a separate piece of paper.

8. Answer the questions below:

   • How many samples did you take before your results matched those of the population?

   _____

   • What were the sizes of your samples? List them and circle the sample that matched.

   _____

   _____

   _____

   • How many matching samples did you obtain? _____

   _____

   • Was the matching sample larger or smaller than you thought it would be? Why?

   _____

   _____

   _____

   _____

   _____

   _____

   _____

Segment Three—Lesson Five (cont.)

Dealing With Data

Translating the Experience

Think about the experience you just had. It was a logical/mathematical experience. You were investigating the relationship between a whole population and a representative sample of that population.

Think about your reaction to the experience. In this part of learning about the multiple intelligences you will be translating logical/mathematical experiences by explaining them in written words. Many people feel that logical/mathematical thinking can be made clear by writing about it.

On the lines below, write about the conclusions you reached while investigating the sampling process. What will you think the next time you hear about the results of a survey? What questions might you want to ask? _____

_____

_____

_____

_____

_____

_____

_____

_____

_____

_____

_____

_____

_____

_____

Segment Three—Lesson Six

Probability

Purpose: to give students the experience of observing and manipulating probability

Skills: knowledge, comprehension, application, analysis, synthesis, and evaluation

Intelligences: logical/mathematical, verbal/linguistic, interpersonal, intrapersonal

Materials:

- heavy paper, scissors, writing and drawing materials, brads for spinners
- copies of "Good Luck!" for each student
- copies of "Spinner Chart" for each student
- copies of "Translating the Experience," one for each student

Procedures:

◆ Have students review the definition of logical/mathematical intelligence.

◆ Introduce this experience with a quick overview of probability. (See the "References" section.)

◆ Pass out "Good Luck!" and "Spinner Chart" sheets. You will probably want students to work in groups (interpersonal) for this activity because it will be more fun. However, if you have students who are comfortable only when working alone (intrapersonal), it could work that way also.

◆ Without any further discussion, ask students to follow the directions on "Good Luck!" and "Spinner Chart."

◆ Then have students work individually on the sheet entitled "Translating the Experience."

◆ Use these sheets for discussion during Evaluation and Processing and then place them in the students' folders.

To Simplify:

Omit "Translating the Experience."

To Expand:

Have students conduct other experiments in probability, such as flipping coins and recording the results (heads or tails) over a number of tries. Encourage students to share their results with the class.

Evaluation and Processing:

Allow students to share and discuss their "Translating the Experience" sheets, as well as their results from "Good Luck!" and "Spinner Chart."

Segment Three—Lesson Six (cont.)

Probability

In this activity you will be experimenting with ways to change your luck in a game.

1. Start by making one "spinner." (See below.) In this case the four numbered sections are equal in size.

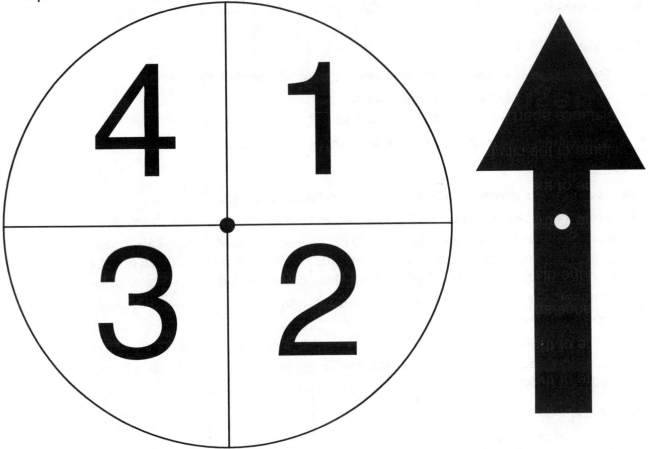

2. Trace the spinner and the arrow on heavy paper and cut them out.

3. Punch a hole in the center of the spinner and in the arrow.

4. Attach the arrow to the spinner with a brad. Make sure it is loose enough to spin around freely.

5. Spin the arrow ten times and record the results on your chart.

6. Make several other spinners like the first one but make the numbered sections different sizes.

7. Spin the arrow ten times for each spinner and record all of the results on your chart.

Segment Three—Lesson Six (cont.)

Probability Chart

After you have prepared the spinner and followed the directions on page 158, use the chart below to record your probability results.

Spins	Spinner #1	Spinner #2	Spinner #3	Spinner #4	Spinner #5
1					
2					
3					
4					
5					
6					
7					
8					
9					
10					

Segment Three—Lesson Six *(cont.)*

Probability

Translating the Experience

Think about the experience you just had. It was a logical/mathematical experience. You were experimenting with ways to change probability.

Think about your reaction to the experience. In this part of learning about the multiple intelligences you will be translating logical/mathematical experiences by explaining them in written words. Many people feel that logical/mathematical thinking can be made clear by writing about it.

On the lines below, write about the conclusions you reached while doing this experiment. What will you look at the next time you play a game of chance? What questions might you want to ask?

Logical/ Mathematical

Segment Three—Lesson Seven

Logic

Purpose: to give students a first-hand experience with patterns

Skills: knowledge, comprehension, application, analysis, synthesis, and evaluation

Intelligences: logical/mathematical, verbal/linguistic, interpersonal, intrapersonal

Materials:

- copies of "Patterns," one for each student
- copies of "Translating the Experience," one for each student

Procedures:

- ◆ Have students review the definition of logical/mathematical intelligence.
- ◆ Introduce this experience with a quick overview of what logic consists of. (See the "References" section.)
- ◆ Pass out "Patterns." You will probably want students to work in groups (interpersonal) for this activity because it would be more enjoyable. However, if you have students who are comfortable only when working alone (intrapersonal), it could work that way also.
- ◆ Without any further discussion, ask students to follow the directions on "Patterns."
- ◆ Then have students work individually on the sheet entitled "Translating the Experience."
- ◆ Use these sheets for discussion during Evaluation and Processing and then place them in the students' folders.

To Simplify:

Omit "Translating the Experience."

To Expand:

Have students look into other areas of logic, such as sorting and classifying. Encourage them to learn and explain the meanings of terms such as attribute, similarity, and difference to the class.

Evaluation and Processing:

Allow students to share and discuss their "Translating the Experience" sheets, as well as their results from "Patterns."

Segment Three—Lesson Seven *(cont.)*

Logic

Patterns

In this activity you will be creating patterns for other students to extend. You, in turn, will solve the patterns created by others. Start your patterns below. One sample pattern is included for you.

Sample: A A B A B C A B C __ __ __ __ __ __

Answer: A A B A B C A B C <u>D</u> <u>A</u> <u>B</u> <u>C</u> <u>D</u> <u>E</u>

1. _____

   _____

2. _____

   _____

3. _____

   _____

4. _____

   _____

5. _____

   _____

6. _____

   _____

7. _____

   _____

8. _____

   _____

Segment Three—Lesson Seven *(cont.)*

Logic

Translating the Experience

Think about the experience you just had. It was a logical/mathematical experience. You were using logic to create, recognize, and extend patterns.

Think about your reaction to the experience. In this part of learning about the multiple intelligences you will be translating logical/mathematical experiences by explaining them in written words. Many people feel that logical/mathematical thinking can be made clear by writing about it.

> On the lines below, write about the conclusions you reached while doing this experiment. For example, what does a pattern have to do before you can extend it?
>
> _____
>
> _____
>
> _____
>
> _____
>
> _____
>
> _____
>
> _____
>
> _____ **A**
>
> _____ **A**
>
> _____ **B**
>
> _____ **A**
>
> _____
>
>   **B**
>
>   **B**   **C**   **B**

Logical/ Mathematical

Segment Three—Lesson Eight

Playing Strategy Games

Purpose: to give students the opportunity to play games associated with logical/mathematical intelligence

Skills: knowledge, comprehension, application, analysis, synthesis, and evaluation

Intelligences: logical/mathematical, interpersonal, intrapersonal

Materials:

- a number of strategy games such as checkers or chess
- copies of "Evaluating the Activity," one for each student
- writing materials

Procedures:

◆ Have students review the definition of logical/mathematical intelligence. (See page 95.)

◆ Ask them to choose a strategy game and begin.

◆ Allow time for students to complete an evaluation at the end of the activity.

◆ Place evaluation sheets in students' folders.

To Simplify:

Allow students to work with an aide or helper, if they wish.

To Expand:

Keep games and puzzles on hand for use during activity times.

Evaluation and Processing:

Share and discuss evaluation sheets.

Segment Three—Lesson Eight *(cont.)*

Playing Strategy Games

Evaluate the activity in which you participated by responding to the following questions.

1. Which game did you play?

   _____

   _____

2. If you were playing with a group, will you continue the game later?

   _____

3. If you were working alone, will you finish later?

   _____

   _____

4. Would you ever play this game outside of school? Where? When?

   _____

   _____

   _____

   _____

5. Is there another type of game that you prefer? What is it?

   _____

   _____

   _____

   _____

Rate this activity from 1 to 10, with 10 being best (circle choice):

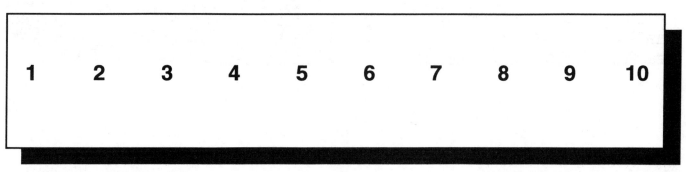

| 1 | 2 | 3 | 4 | 5 | 6 | 7 | 8 | 9 | 10 |

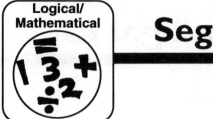

Segment Three—Lesson Nine

Sharing Translations

Purpose: to give students the opportunity to share their various translations from logical/mathematical to verbal/linguistic intelligence

Skills: knowledge, comprehension, application, analysis, synthesis, and evaluation

Intelligences: logical/mathematical, verbal/linguistic, interpersonal, intrapersonal

Materials:

- individual student folders

Procedures:

- ◆ Invite students to share the translations from logical/mathematical to verbal/linguistic intelligence they made during this segment.
- ◆ Allow time for presentations and positive acknowledgements of effort.

To Simplify:

Allow students to work with an aide or helper if they wish.

To Expand:

Encourage students to use on future assignments the techniques they learned in this segment.

Evaluation and Processing:

This activity is actually an evaluation and processing of the entire segment.

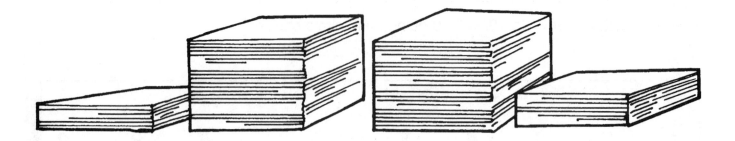

Segment Four—Nine Lessons

From the Middle of January Through the First Week of February

During the fourth segment of this minicurriculum, students will have their third experience with archetypal examples of the intelligences, as we consider the visual/spatial.

Visual/spatial intelligence means thinking in pictures—learning through visual experiences, expressing ideas and feelings through art, and having fun solving mazes and putting together jigsaw puzzles.

The topics in this segment will include suggestions for exposing students to archetypal examples of visual/spatial intelligence, such as paintings, sculpture, and architecture. The topics will also provide opportunities to learn from visual presentations and to apply this intelligence to activities using models, maps, diagrams, and games. Pretending, imagining, and manipulating mental models will also be included.

The topics selected for this segment are listed below. Brief descriptions and/or explanations follow for your convenience. You may wish to refresh your own familiarity with them. You should, of course, feel free to substitute or add your own favorite topics. If this is "your" intelligence, you will have favorite topics that make this area come alive for you.

1. **The Graphic Arts**

2. **Sculpture**

3. **Architecture**

4. **Maps and Diagrams**

5. **Movies and Television**

6. **Demonstrations Using Models and Props**

7. **Pretending, Imagining, and Manipulating Mental Models**

8. **Playing Visual/Spatial Games**

9. **Sharing Translations**

Calendars for Segment Four

Directions: Use the calendars below to plan when you would like to do the nine lessons of this segment. The lessons are listed on the previous page. The highlighted weeks are the time periods which are suggested.

January

M	T	W	T	F
		S e g m e n t F o u r		
		S e g m e n t F o u r		

February

M	T	W	T	F
		S e g m e n t F o u r		

Segment Four

References

1. The Graphic Arts

Painting is one of the most important of the graphic arts. Painting is done in oils, watercolors, tempera, etc., and applied to many surfaces, including, most commonly, canvas. When a painting is done directly on a wall, it is called a mural.

A painting can be . . .

- a portrait
- a landscape
- a still life
- an abstract

There are many styles of painting:

- cubism
- expressionism
- impressionism
- naturalism
- primitivism
- realism
- romanticism
- surrealism

2. Sculpture

Sculpture is three-dimensional art created from wood, stone, clay, or metal.

Types of sculpture:

- statues
- busts
- reliefs
- bas-reliefs
- mobiles

Some famous sculptors:

- Michelangelo (*David, Pieta*)
- Rodin (*The Thinker*)
- Bartholdi (*Statue of Liberty*)
- Calder (mobiles)
- Moore (massive stone sculptures)

Segment Four (cont.)

References (cont.)

2. Sculpture *(cont.)*

Some famous statues by unknown artists are:

- *the Sphinx*
- *Venus de Milo*
- *Nike of Samothrace (Winged Victory)*

3. Architecture

Architecture is the art of designing buildings and other structures, such as walls and towers.

Some famous examples of ancient architecture:

- the Pyramids (Egypt)
- the Parthenon (Athens)
- the Colosseum (Rome)
- the Great Wall (China)

Famous buildings of more recent times include:

- St. Peter's Basilica (Vatican City)
- Leaning Tower of Pisa (Italy)
- The Taj Mahal (Agra)

Famous modern buildings:

- Monticello (Thomas Jefferson's home in Virginia)
- The Eiffel Tower (Paris)
- The Empire State Building (New York)
- The World Trade Center (New York)
- The Sears Tower (Chicago—the world's tallest building)

Some styles of architecture:

- Doric
- Ionic
- Corinthian
- Gothic
- Romanesque

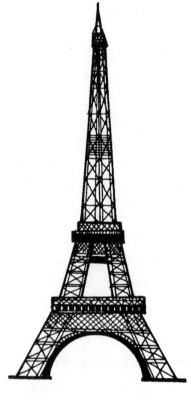

Segment Four *(cont.)*

References *(cont.)*

4. Maps and Diagrams

Maps are simplified pictures that generally show areas on the surface of the earth. You can also find maps of the moon, as well as maps of fictional places.

The various types of maps:

- physical maps
- political maps
- product maps
- road maps

Diagrams are drawings that explain how something works by showing its parts and their relationships.

Diagrams can be amusing, as well as useful. Rube Goldberg was, and still is, famous for his drawings of complicated machines that were designed to accomplish simple or useless tasks.

5. Movies and Television

The media are all the means of communication, such as newspapers, radio, movies, and TV, that provide news and entertainment for the general public.

Movies and TV are visual media. Much of their communication is done with pictures.

The early movies, which were "silent" films, were completely visual experiences. In the early twentieth century, Charlie Chaplin created silent comedies in which he played the Little Tramp, his most famous character. Some of Chaplin's best-known films are *The Gold Rush, City Lights,* and *Modern Times.*

6. Demonstrations Using Models and Props

Models and props are visual aids that help people understand the ideas being expressed in oral communication. The use of these visual aids turns a lecture into a demonstration (an explanation by example).

7. Pretending, Imagining, and Manipulating Mental Models

8. Playing Visual/Spatial Games

- mazes
- jigsaw puzzles

9. Sharing Translations

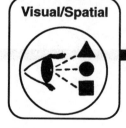

Visual/Spatial

Segment Four—Lesson One

The Graphic Arts

Purpose: to expose students to examples of some of the world's greatest paintings

Skills: knowledge, comprehension, application, analysis, synthesis, and evaluation

Intelligences: Potentially all may be involved.

Materials:

- large art prints of all different periods, types, and painting styles (These may be available for check-out from your district media center or library. If not, you can use books of prints which should be available in any library.)
- copies of "Translating the Experience," one for each student

Procedures:

- ◆ Turn your room into an art gallery by displaying as many large prints of paintings as possible or supply each group with several books of art prints.
- ◆ Have students review the definition of visual/spatial intelligence.
- ◆ Introduce this experience by discussing the various types and styles of painting. (See the "References" section.)
- ◆ Let students browse through the books or walk around and study the prints. Students may work in groups (interpersonal) or alone (intrapersonal); it is up to you and will probably depend on whether you use large prints on the walls or books of prints.
- ◆ Allow plenty of time for looking at the paintings. Then, without any further discussion, ask students to work individually on the sheet entitled "Translating the Experience."
- ◆ Use these sheets for discussion during Evaluation and Processing and then place them in the students' folders.

To Simplify:

Omit "Translating the Experience."

To Expand:

Ask students to choose a style of painting to research. Encourage them to share what they discover with the rest of the class.

Evaluation and Processing:

Allow students to share and discuss their "Translating the Experience" sheets.

Segment Four—Lesson One *(cont.)*

The Graphic Arts

Translating the Experience

Think about the experience you just had. It was a visual/spatial experience. You looked at a print of something someone had painted.

Think about your reaction to the experience. Decide how you could translate your reaction by expressing it through another of the intelligences. Do not express your reaction through your visual/spatial intelligence!

Which intelligence will you use to translate your experience?

_____

What materials, if any, will you need?

_____   _____

_____   _____

_____   _____

Will you need time to prepare your translation?

_____

How much? How will you share your translation with the class?

_____

_____

_____

_____

_____

_____

_____

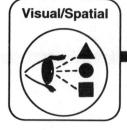

Visual/Spatial

Segment Four—Lesson Two

Sculpture

Purpose: to expose students to examples of some of the world's greatest sculptures

Skills: knowledge, comprehension, application, analysis, synthesis, and evaluation

Intelligences: visual/spatial, bodily/kinesthetic, verbal/linguistic, interpersonal, intrapersonal

Materials:

- large art prints of all different periods, types, and styles of sculpture (These may be available for check-out from your district media center or library. If not, you can use books of prints which should be available in any library.)
- clay, enough for everyone to have a good-sized chunk
- tools such as tongue depressors, plastic picnic knives, craft sticks
- copies of "Translating the Experience," one for each student

Procedures:

- ◆ If possible, take your students to an art gallery or sculpture garden where they can see sculpture in three-dimension instead of as flat pictures in a book.
- ◆ Turn your room into a gallery by displaying as many large prints of sculptures as possible or supply each group with several books of sculpture prints.
- ◆ Have students review the definition of visual/spatial intelligence.
- ◆ Introduce this experience by discussing the various types of sculpture and some of the most famous sculptors. (See the "References" section.)
- ◆ Let students browse through the books or walk around and study the prints. Students may work in groups (interpersonal) or alone (intrapersonal); it is up to you, and it will probably depend on whether you use large prints on the walls or books of prints.
- ◆ Allow plenty of time for looking at the sculptures. Then, without any further discussion, pass out the clay and the tools and ask students to work individually, referring to the sheet entitled "Translating the Experience."
- ◆ Use these sheets for discussion during Evaluation and Processing and then place them in the students' folders.

To Simplify:

Allow students to work with aides or parent helpers.

To Expand:

Encourage students to choose a type of sculpture to research.

Evaluation and Processing:

Allow students to share and discuss their "Translating the Experience" sheets.

Segment Four—Lesson Two *(cont.)*

Sculpture

Translating the Experience

Think about the experience you just had. It was a visual/spatial experience. You looked at a print of a sculpture that someone had shaped from a material of some kind.

Looking at sculpture is a visual/spatial experience; creating the sculpture is a visual/spatial experience too, because the sculptor must see the picture of what is being created in his or her mind. However, it is also a bodily/kinesthetic experience, because the sculptor must use his or her hands to shape the sculpture.

In order to fully experience sculpture, you are going to have a chance to make something out of clay with your hands, thus translating a visual/spatial experience into a bodily/kinesthetic one. Finally, when you answer the questions below about the process, you will be using your verbal/linguistic intelligence.

Using Your Clay to Make Something

What effect did it have on you when you translated your visual/spatial experience into a bodily/kinesthetic experience?

_____

_____

_____

_____

Which use of intelligence feels more natural to you?

- Visual/Spatial—looking at sculpture
- Bodily/Kinesthetic—creating sculpture
- Verbal/Linguistic—turning the experience into words

Why?_____

_____

_____

_____

_____

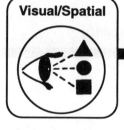

Visual/Spatial

Segment Four—Lesson Three

Architecture

Purpose: to expose students to examples of some of the world's greatest architecture

Skills: knowledge, comprehension, application, analysis, synthesis, and evaluation

Intelligences: Potentially all may be involved.

Materials:

- large art prints of famous buildings of different periods (These may be available for check-out from your district media center or library. If not, you can use books of prints which should be available in any library.)
- copies of "Translating the Experience," one for each student

Procedures:

◆ If possible, take your students to look at outstanding or unusual buildings in your area so that they can experience architecture "in person" and not by flat pictures in a book.

◆ Turn your room into a gallery by displaying as many large prints of architecture as possible or supply each group with several books of architecture prints.

◆ Have students review the definition of visual/spatial intelligence.

◆ Introduce this experience by discussing some famous examples of architecture. (See the "References" section.)

◆ Let students browse through the books or walk around and study the prints. Students may work in groups (interpersonal) or alone (intrapersonal); it is up to you and will probably depend on whether you use large prints on the walls or books of prints.

◆ Allow plenty of time for looking at the prints. Then, without any further discussion, have students work on the sheet entitled "Translating the Experience."

◆ Use these sheets for discussion during Evaluation and Processing and then place them in the students' folders.

To Simplify:

Omit "Translating the Experience."

To Expand:

Ask students to choose a type of architecture to research. Encourage them to report the results of their research to the class.

Evaluation and Processing:

Allow students to share and discuss their "Translating the Experience" sheets.

Segment Four—Lesson Three *(cont.)*

Architecture

Translating the Experience

Think about the experience you just had. It was a visual/spatial experience. You looked at a print of something someone had built.

Think about your reaction to the experience. Decide how you could translate your reaction by expressing it through another one of the intelligences. Do not express your reaction through your visual/spatial intelligence!

Which intelligence will you use to translate your experience?

_____

What materials, if any, will you need?

_____   _____

_____   _____

_____   _____

Will you need time to prepare your translation? How much?

_____

How will you share your translation with the class?

_____

_____

_____

_____

_____

_____

_____

_____

_____

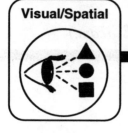

Visual/Spatial

Segment Four—Lesson Four

Maps and Diagrams

Purpose: to give students the experience of viewing and creating an amusing type of diagram

Skills: knowledge, comprehension, application, analysis, synthesis, and evaluation

Intelligences: visual/spatial, bodily/kinesthetic, interpersonal, intrapersonal

Materials:

- examples of some of Rube Goldberg's cartoon diagrams of imaginary inventions (Collections containing examples of Rube Goldberg's work should be available in any library.)
- copies of "Translating the Experience," one for each student

Procedures:

- ◆ Provide examples of Rube Goldberg's cartoon diagrams for groups and/or individual students.
- ◆ Have students review the definition of visual/spatial intelligence.
- ◆ Give a brief introduction to Rube Goldberg and his work. (See the "References" section, page 171.)
- ◆ Let students enjoy looking at and discussing the various diagrams. Students may work in groups (interpersonal) or alone (intrapersonal).
- ◆ Allow plenty of time for looking at the diagrams. Then, without any further discussion, have students work on the sheet entitled "Translating the Experience."
- ◆ Use these sheets for discussion during Evaluation and Processing and then place them in the students' folders.

To Simplify:

Allow students to work with aides or parent helpers.

To Expand:

Encourage students to make additional diagrams for fun. Post them around the room for everyone to enjoy.

Evaluation and Processing:

Allow students to share and discuss their diagrams, as well as their "Translating the Experience" sheets.

Segment Four—Lesson Four *(cont.)*

Maps and Diagrams

Translating the Experience

Think about the experience you just had. It was a visual/spatial experience. You looked at a print of a humorous diagram—something someone had drawn.

Looking at a diagram is a visual/spatial experience; creating the diagram is a visual/spatial experience also, because the artist must see the picture of what is being created in his or her mind. However, it is also a bodily/kinesthetic experience, because the artist must use his or her hands to draw the diagram.

In order to fully experience these diagrams, you are going to have a chance to draw one of your own with your hands, thus translating a visual/spatial experience into a bodily/kinesthetic one. Finally, when you answer the questions below about the process, you will be using your verbal/linguistic intelligence.

Visual/Spatial: First, think of a Rube-Goldberg-type job (a very simple task).

Second, imagine a complicated machine to do that task.

Bodily/Kinesthetic: Draw a diagram of the machine, showing how it works.

Verbal/Linguistic: Now answer the questions below.

How did it affect you when you translated your visual/spatial experience into a bodily/kinesthetic experience? _____

_____

_____

Which use of intelligence feels more natural to you?_____

_____

- Visual/Spatial—looking at a diagram
- Bodily/Kinesthetic—creating a diagram
- Verbal/Linguistic—turning the experience into words

Why?_____

_____

_____

_____

MY Invention

BY Natalie

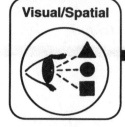

Visual/Spatial

Segment Four—Lesson Five

Movies and Television

Purpose: to expose students to a classic example of an early motion picture

Skills: knowledge, comprehension, application, analysis, synthesis, and evaluation

Intelligences: Potentially all may be involved.

Materials:

- one of Charlie Chaplin's early movies and a projector (or use a video taped version, a TV, and a VCR)
- copies of "Translating the Experience," one for each student

Procedures:

◆ Have students review the definition of visual/spatial intelligence.

◆ Give a brief introduction of silent films and of Charlie Chaplin and his work. (See the "Reference" section.)

◆ Show one of Chaplin's silent films. (As with any outside film sources, obtain the necessary district permission before viewing.)

◆ Without any further discussion, have students work on the sheet entitled "Translating the Experience."

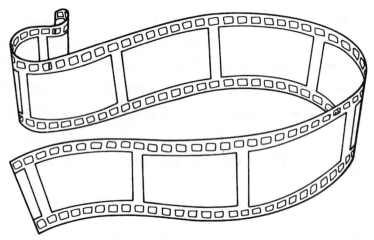

◆ Use these sheets for discussion during Evaluation and Processing and then place them in the students' folders.

To Simplify:

Omit "Translating the Experience."

To Expand:

Encourage students to find out more about early film making.

Evaluation and Processing:

Allow students to share and discuss their "Translating the Experience" sheets.

Segment Four—Lesson Five (cont.)

Movies and Television

Translating the Experience

Think about the experience you just had. It was a visual/spatial experience. You looked at a silent film.

Think about your reaction to the experience. Decide how you could translate your reaction by expressing it through another one of the intelligences. Do not express your reaction through your visual/spatial intelligence!

Which intelligence will you use to translate your experience?

_____

What materials, if any, will you need?

_____   _____

_____   _____

_____

Will you need time to prepare your translation? How much?

_____

How will you share your translation with the class?

_____

_____

_____

_____

_____

_____

_____

_____

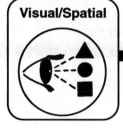

Visual/Spatial

Segment Four—Lesson Six

Demonstrations Using Models and Props

Purpose: to give students the experience of demonstrations, using models and props

Skills: knowledge, comprehension, application, analysis, synthesis, and evaluation

Intelligences: visual/spatial, bodily/kinesthetic, interpersonal, intrapersonal

Materials:

- two sets of copies of "Partner Assignments"
- copies of "Translating the Experience," one for each student

Procedures:

- ◆ Review "Partner Assignments" ahead of time. On one set of these pages assign and write in the names of the students on the appropriate lines. Fill in and keep the second set of "Partner Assignments" as a master copy for yourself.
- ◆ Assemble any necessary props. (You may need to ask students to bring things from home.)
- ◆ Have students review the definition of visual/spatial intelligence.
- ◆ Cut the "Partner Assignments" into slips and pass them out to the students.
- ◆ Explain to the students that both partners will be giving separate demonstrations of the same thing. One student will use props and words, while the other student will only be able to use words.
- ◆ Have students get together with their partners and plan their demonstrations.
- ◆ Have each partner/pair make their presentation.
- ◆ Without any further discussion, have students work on the sheet entitled "Translating the Experience."
- ◆ Use these sheets for discussion during Evaluation and Processing and then place them in the students' folders.

To Simplify:

Allow students to work with aides or parent helpers.

To Expand:

Encourage students to develop other demonstrations or to report on demonstrations that have helped them learn how to do something.

Evaluation and Processing:

Allow students to share and discuss their "Translating the Experience" sheets.

Segment Four—Lesson Six *(cont.)*

Demonstrations Using Models and Props

Partner Assignments

Below are the assignments for the partner demonstrations. One student will give an explanation of a topic just in words, without using a model or a prop. The other student will explain the same topic with the use of a model or a prop. You may decide who will do each part.

How to Ride a Bicycle   _____

_____

How to Ride a Skateboard   _____

_____

How to Draw a Triangle   _____

_____

How to Thread a Needle   _____

_____

How to Cover a Book   _____

_____

How to Rollerblade   _____

_____

Segment Four—Lesson Six *(cont.)*

Demonstrations Using Models and Props

Partner Assignments *(cont.)*

How to Find a Page in a Book by Using an Index

_____

_____

How to Use a Compass in Geometry

_____

_____

How to Open a Carton of Milk

_____

_____

How to Put on a Sweatshirt

_____

_____

How to Turn on a Computer

_____

_____

How to Find a Word in a Dictionary

_____

_____

Segment Four—Lesson Six (cont.)

Demonstrations Using Models and Props

Partner Assignments (cont.)

How to Lace and Tie a Shoe

_____

_____

How to Braid Hair

_____

_____

How to Fasten a Button

_____

_____

How to Open a Pop-Top Can

_____

_____

How to Roll Up a Sleeping Bag

_____

_____

How to Inflate and Tie a Balloon

_____

_____

Segment Four—Lesson Six *(cont.)*

Demonstrations Using Models and Props

Translating the Experience

Think about the experience you just had. In some ways it was a visual/spatial experience. You looked at demonstrations given with and without the use of models and props. However, it was also a bodily/kinesthetic experience. You gave a demonstration either with or without the use of models or props.

Think about your reaction to this experience and answer the questions below.

Which demonstrations were the easiest to understand, the ones with props or without? Explain. _____

_____

_____

_____

If you used a prop, how did you feel during your demonstration?

_____

_____

_____

If you did not use a prop, how did you feel during your demonstration? _____

_____

_____

_____

_____

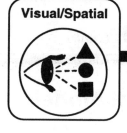

Visual/Spatial

Segment Four—Lesson Seven

Pretending, Imagining, and Manipulating
Mental Models

Purpose: to give students the opportunity to pretend, imagine, and manipulate mental models

Skills: knowledge, comprehension, application, analysis, synthesis, and evaluation

Intelligences: Potentially all may be involved.

Materials:

- sets of water color paints and brushes, one for each student
- white drawing paper
- copies of "Translating the Experience," one for each student

Procedures:

◆ Have students review the definition of visual/spatial intelligence.

◆ Distribute paints, brushes, and paper.

◆ Ask students to paint something (e.g., a picture, design, or abstract impression) that reflects their own experience with any or all of the aspects of visual/spatial intelligence which they have experienced during this segment.

◆ Without any further discussion, have students work on the sheet entitled "Translating the Experience."

◆ Use these sheets for discussion during Evaluation and Processing and then place them in the students' folders.

To Simplify:

Allow students to work with aides or parent helpers.

To Expand:

Encourage students to further develop their paintings or create additional paintings to express their visual/spatial intelligence.

Evaluation and Processing:

Allow students to share and discuss their "Translating the Experience" sheets, as well as their paintings which can be displayed in the classroom.

Note:

Visual/spatial intelligence is related to bodily/kinesthetic intelligence because the pictures in the mind are often expressed through the mechanism of the body.

Segment Four—Lesson Seven (cont.)

Pretending, Imagining, and Manipulating Mental Models

Translating the Experience

Think about the experience you just had. It was a visual/spatial experience. You expressed your mental impressions as a painting.

Think about your reaction to the experience. Decide which one of the other intelligences was involved in this experience. Decide how you could translate your reaction by expressing it through still another one of the intelligences.

Which intelligence, other than visual/spatial, was involved in this experience? What is the relationship between visual/spatial intelligence and this other intelligence?

Which additional intelligence will you use to translate your experience?_____

_____

What materials, if any, will you need?

_____   _____

_____   _____

_____   _____

Will you need time to prepare your translation? How much?

_____

How will you share your translation with the class?_____

_____

_____

_____

_____

_____

_____

_____

_____

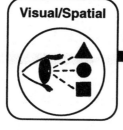

Visual/Spatial

Segment Four—Lesson Eight

Playing Spatial Games

Purpose: to give students the opportunity to play games associated with visual/spatial intelligence

Skills: knowledge, comprehension, application, analysis, synthesis, and evaluation

Intelligences: visual/spatial, interpersonal, intrapersonal

Materials:

- a number of games, such as mazes and jigsaw puzzles
- copies of "Evaluating the Activity," one for each student
- writing materials

Procedures:

◆ Have students review the definition of visual/spatial intelligence.

◆ Ask them to choose an activity and begin.

◆ Allow time for students to complete an evaluation at the end of the activity.

◆ Place the evaluation sheets in the students' folders.

To Simplify:

Allow students to work with an aide or helper, if they wish.

To Expand:

Keep games and puzzles on hand for use during activity times.

Evaluation and Processing:

Share and discuss evaluation sheets.

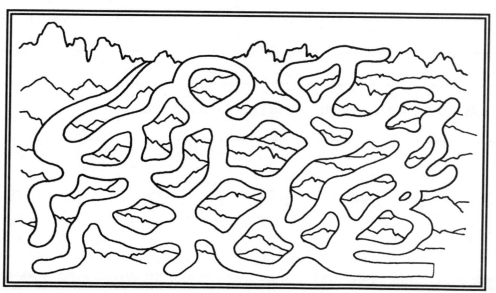

Segment Four—Lesson Eight *(cont.)*

Playing Spatial Games

Evaluate the activity on page 189 by responding to the following questions.

1. Which game did you play?

   _____

   _____

2. If you were playing with a group, will you continue the game later?

   _____

   _____

3. If you were working alone, will you finish later?

   _____

   _____

4. Would you ever play this game outside of school? Where? When?

   _____

   _____

   _____

5. Is there another type of game that you prefer? What is it?

   _____

   _____

   _____

   _____

Rate this activity from 1 to 10, with10 being best (*circle choice*):

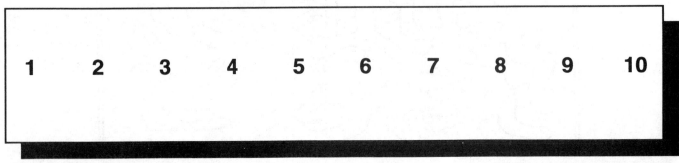

| 1 | 2 | 3 | 4 | 5 | 6 | 7 | 8 | 9 | 10 |

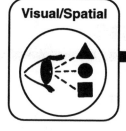

Visual/Spatial

Segment Four—Lesson Nine

Sharing Translations

Purpose: to give students the opportunity to share their translations from visual/spatial to various other intelligences

Skills: knowledge, comprehension, application, analysis, synthesis, and evaluation

Intelligences: Potentially all may be involved.

Materials:

- individual student folders

Procedures:

◆ Invite students to share the translations from visual/spatial to any other intelligence they made or planned during this segment.

◆ Allow time for presentations and positive acknowledgements of effort.

To Simplify:

Allow students to work with an aide or helper, if they wish.

To Expand:

Encourage students to use the techniques they learned in this segment on future assignments.

Evaluation and Processing:

This activity is actually an evaluation and processing of the entire segment.

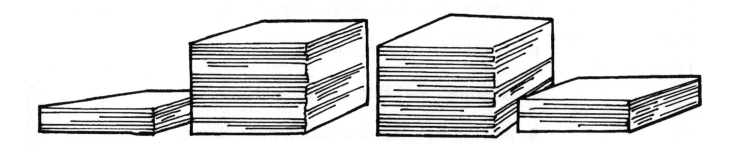

Segment Five—Nine Lessons

From the Middle of February Through the First Week of March

During the fifth segment of this minicurriculum, students will have a fourth experience with archetypal examples of the intelligences as we consider the bodily/kinesthetic.

Body/kinesthetic intelligence means thinking through touch and movement—acting things out, manipulating objects, and using both large and small muscles in physical activities and sports of all kinds. People with this kind of intelligence process information through the sensations they feel in their bodies and express emotion and mood through dance. They enjoy games that require excellent eye/hand coordination.

The topics in this segment will include suggestions for exposing students to archetypal examples of bodily/kinesthetic experience (dance, acting, professional sports), as well as affording opportunities to use manipulative materials and build things, engage in physical activities, and observe and practice gestures and other body language.

The topics selected for this segment are listed below. Brief descriptions and/or explanations follow for your convenience. You may wish to refresh your own familiarity with them. You should, of course, feel free to substitute or add your own favorite topics. If this is "your" intelligence, you will have favorite topics that make this area come alive for you.

1. **Dance**

2. **Acting**

3. **Professional Sports**

4. **Using Manipulatives**

5. **Making Models and Building Things**

6. **Exercise and Athletics**

7. **Gestures and Body Language**

8. **Playing Eye/Hand Coordination Games**

9. **Sharing Translations**

Calendars for Segment Five

Directions: Use the calendars below to plan when you would like to do the nine lessons of this segment. The lessons are listed on the previous page. The highlighted weeks are the time periods which are suggested.

February

M	T	W	T	F
		Segment Five		
		Segment Five		

March

M	T	W	T	F
		Segment Five		

Segment Five

References

1. Dance

Dance is one of the performing arts. In dance, rhythmic movements of the feet and body are made, usually in time to music.

Types of dance:

- ballet
- modern dance
- jazz
- tap
- ballroom

Famous ballets include *Swan Lake, Sleeping Beauty*, and *The Nutcracker*—all of which were written by Peter Tchaikovsky, a nineteenth century Russian composer.

2. Acting

Acting is one of the performing arts. In acting, people assume roles and portray them for audiences on radio, in movies and TV, and on the stage.

Although actors certainly use their voices, they also use a variety of different physical and bodily/kinesthetic techniques to give the audience information about the characters they are portraying. These techniques include:

- posture
- gestures
- facial expressions
- speed of movement
- emotional attitude
- costumes
- special effects makeup

3. Professional Sports

Highly paid professional sports in the United States:

- baseball
- basketball
- football
- hockey

Although professional sports are true bodily/kinesthetic experiences only to the athletes who participate in them, they often become vicarious bodily/kinesthetic experiences for spectators.

Segment Five *(cont.)*

References *(cont.)*

4. Using Manipulatives

Manipulatives are small objects that can be handled conveniently and used for some educational purpose. They are often used for counting and for helping students see clearly what is happening during the processes of adding and subtracting. If manipulatives are to be used in a classroom, they should be safe and easy to store.

Some manipulatives used in a classroom:

- blocks
- buttons
- craft sticks
- coins

5. Making Models and Building Things

Making models and building (or fixing) things is easy and enjoyable for people with bodily/kinesthetic intelligence. You may never know whether or not you have this type of intelligence until you give it a try.

People who try for the first time to make or build something may find that they have an intelligence they never suspected, or they may find that they have very little skill in this area. Even with very little natural skill, it is possible to become competent in making or fixing things with your hands. You may never enjoy it, but you can at least become skillful enough to make minor repairs in case of an emergency.

6. Exercise and Athletics

Exercise can be done to . . .

- build the cardio-vascular system (aerobics)
- increase muscle strength (weight training)
- increase flexibility (stretching)

Athletics . . .

- are sports, games, and exercises requiring strength, speed, agility, etc.
- consist of activities that are pursued for fun or practiced competitively rather than for money

Segment Five *(cont.)*

References *(cont.)*

7. Gestures and Body Language

Body language, including the gestures made by the hands, is not only a type of communication tool, it is also a part of cultural diversity.

Samples of body language:

- establishment of personal space
- ways of showing respect
- different kinds of table manners
- acceptable types of eye contact

There are even places in this world where the up-and-down nod of the head means "no" and the side-to-side shake means "yes."

8. Playing Eye/Hand Coordination Games

- interactive computer games
- Sega/Genesis®
- Nintendo®

9. Sharing Translations

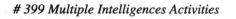

Bodily/ Kinesthetic

Segment Five—Lesson One

Dance

Purpose: to give students experience with the elements of dance

Skills: knowledge, comprehension, application, analysis, synthesis, and evaluation

Intelligences: Potentially all may be involved.

Materials:

- a movie or video of a well-known ballet (Since students are probably more familiar with other forms of dance, ballet may provide a more memorable experience.)
- copies of "The Five Basic Positions in Ballet," one for each student
- copies of "Translating the Experience," one for each student

Procedures:

- ◆ Have students review the definition of bodily/kinesthetic intelligence.
- ◆ Introduce this experience by giving a brief overview of dance as a performing art. (See the "References" section.)
- ◆ Show the movie or video of the ballet.
- ◆ Pass out "The Five Basic Positions in Ballet" and allow the students to try this bodily/kinesthetic experience. If anyone in the class has taken ballet, he or she can help. Students may work in groups or as partners (interpersonal) or alone (intrapersonal).
- ◆ Then, without any further discussion, ask students to work individually on the sheet entitled "Translating the Experience."
- ◆ Use these sheets for discussion during Evaluation and Processing and then place them in the students' folders.

To Simplify:

Allow students to work with aides or parent helpers.

To Expand:

Ask students to look for other videos that include dance sequences. These can later be shared with the class. Contrast different types of dance. Suggest movies that star Fred Astaire or Gene Kelly.

Evaluation and Processing:

Allow students to share and discuss their "Translating the Experience" sheets.

Segment Five—Lesson One (cont.)

Dance

The Five Basic Positions in Ballet

Practice the five basic ballet positions shown below. Work with a partner or in a group to help each other. If there is a mirror in your classroom, observe yourself.

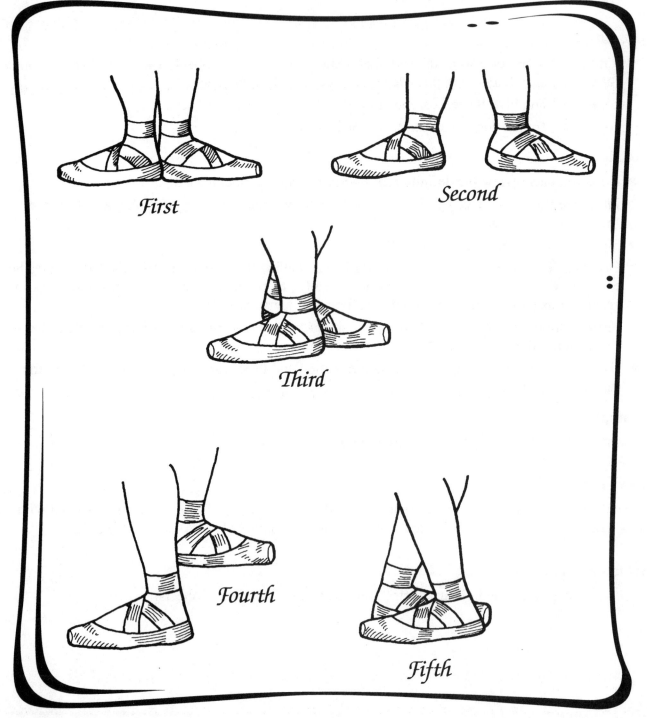

First

Second

Third

Fourth

Fifth

Segment Five—Lesson One *(cont.)*

Dance

Translating the Experience

Think about the experience you just had. At first, it was a visual/spatial experience because you were watching other people dance. You did not begin to have a bodily/kinesthetic experience until you used your body to try the ballet positions yourself.

Think about your reaction to the experience. Decide how you could translate your reaction by expressing it through another one of the intelligences. Try not to use either the bodily/kinesthetic or visual/spatial intelligences.

Which intelligence will you use to translate your experience?

_____

What materials, if any, will you need?

_____   _____

_____   _____

_____   _____

Will you need time to prepare your translation? How much?

_____

How will you share your translation with the class?

_____

_____

_____

_____

_____

_____

_____

_____

Bodily/ Kinesthetic

Segment Five—Lesson Two

Acting

Purpose: to give students experience with some of the bodily/kinesthetic elements of acting

Skills: knowledge, comprehension, application, analysis, synthesis, and evaluation

Intelligences: Potentially all may be involved.

Materials:

- copies of pages 201–208, randomly distributed, one to each student
- copies of "Acting Evaluation," several for each student, with extras
- copies of "Translating the Experience," one for each student

Procedures:

◆ Have students review the definition of bodily/kinesthetic intelligence.

◆ Introduce this experience by giving a brief overview of acting. (See the "References" section.)

◆ Randomly pass out pages 201–208, one to each student. If students are working in groups (interpersonal), make sure each person in a group gets a different character sheet.

◆ Give students time to figure out (and discuss) how to portray their characters.

◆ Call on volunteers to perform. If you have enough time, encourage everyone to take part.

◆ Have the members of the audience (other student groups) fill out the "Acting Evaluation" forms for each performance.

◆ Then, without any further discussion, ask students to work individually on the sheet entitled "Translating the Experience."

◆ Use these sheets for discussion during Evaluation and Processing and then place them in the students' folders.

To Simplify:

Allow students to work with aides or parent helpers.

To Expand:

Encourage students to apply what they have learned in this lesson to real life in the classroom. (For example, "From the way Gina walks, I think she is sad.")

Evaluation and Processing:

Allow students to share and discuss their "Translating the Experience" sheets, as well as their "Acting Evaluation" forms.

Segment Five—Lesson Two *(cont.)*

Acting

Character #1

Your task in this activity is to portray the character described below so that your audience (your classmates) will know as much as possible about him or her. You cannot speak in this exercise, and you will not have the help of costumes or makeup, so you must achieve your effect solely with the bodily/kinesthetic elements of acting.

Do not show your character description to anyone.

Character Description

This character is an old man who has arthritis. He is in pain, but he tries to project a cheerful mood. He is walking down the street in the small town where he has lived all of his life, making his way to the general store.

Things to Consider

How will you make him (yourself) look old? _____

_____

_____

How will you make him (yourself) look as if he is in pain? (Arthritis affects the joints.)

_____

_____

How will you express his attempt to be cheerful?_____

_____

_____

How will you get across the idea that he is in the small town where he has always lived?

_____

_____

_____

_____

Segment Five—Lesson Two *(cont.)*

Acting

Character #2

Your task in this activity is to portray the character described below so that your audience (your classmates) will know as much as possible about him or her. You cannot speak in this exercise, and you will not have the help of costumes or makeup, so you must achieve your effect solely with the bodily/kinesthetic elements of acting.

Do not show your character description to anyone.

Character Description

This character is an old man who has arthritis. He is in pain, and he does not care who knows it. He is walking down the street in the small town where he has lived all his life, making his way to the general store.

Things to Consider

How will you make him (yourself) look old? _____

_____

_____

How will you make him (yourself) look as if he is in pain? (Arthritis affects the joints.)

_____

_____

How will you express his attitude? (No words, remember.)_____

_____

_____

How will you get across the idea that he is in the small town where he has always lived?

_____

_____

_____

Segment Five—Lesson Two *(cont.)*

Acting

Character #3

Your task in this activity is to portray the character described below so that your audience (your classmates) will know as much as possible about him or her. You cannot speak in this exercise, and you will not have the help of costumes or makeup, so you must achieve your effect solely with the bodily/kinesthetic elements of acting.

Do not show your character description to anyone.

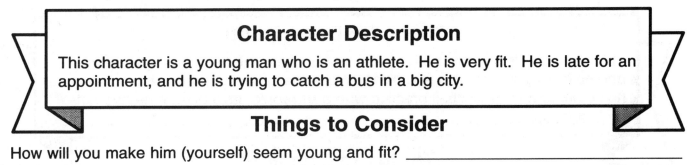

Character Description

This character is a young man who is an athlete. He is very fit. He is late for an appointment, and he is trying to catch a bus in a big city.

Things to Consider

How will you make him (yourself) seem young and fit? _____

_____

_____

How will you make him (yourself) look as if he is in a hurry? _____

_____

_____

How will you get across the idea that he is trying to catch a bus? _____

_____

_____

_____

How will you let the audience know that he is in a big city? _____

_____

_____

_____

_____

Segment Five—Lesson Two *(cont.)*

Acting

Character #4

Your task in this activity is to portray the character described below so that your audience (your classmates) will know as much as possible about him or her. You cannot speak in this exercise, and you will not have the help of costumes or makeup, so you must achieve your effect solely with the bodily/kinesthetic elements of acting.

Do not show your character description to anyone.

Character Description

This character is a young man who is on crutches. He has one leg in a cast, and he is very crabby. He is walking across the school grounds on his way home, instead of to football practice where he would have been if he had not broken his leg.

Things to Consider

How will you make him (yourself) seem young? _____

_____

_____

How will you let the audience know he is on crutches and has a broken leg?

_____

_____

How will you get across the idea that he is walking across the school grounds?

_____

_____

How will you express his attitude? _____

_____

_____

Segment Five—Lesson Two *(cont.)*

Acting

Character #5

Your task in this activity is to portray the character described below so that your audience (your classmates) will know as much as possible about him or her. You cannot speak in this exercise, and you will not have the help of costumes or makeup, so you must achieve your effect solely with the bodily/kinesthetic elements of acting.

Do not show your character description to anyone.

Character Description

This character is a middle-aged woman. She is carrying a baby and has two other small children with her. She seems very stressed as she comes out of a store with a shopping cart full of groceries.

Things to Consider

How will you make her (yourself) seem middle-aged? _____

_____

_____

How will you make her (yourself) look as if she is carrying a baby and has two other children with her? _____

_____

_____

How will you let the audience know where she is and what she is doing?

_____

_____

_____

How will you express her attitude? _____

_____

_____

Segment Five—Lesson Two *(cont.)*

Acting

Character #6

Your task in this activity is to portray the character described below so that your audience (your classmates) will know as much as possible about him or her. You cannot speak in this exercise, and you will not have the help of costumes or makeup, so you must achieve your effect solely with the bodily/kinesthetic elements of acting.

Do not show your character description to anyone.

Character Description

This character is a middle-aged woman. She is carrying a baby and has two other small children with her. They are at the beach, and she seems very happy as they run in and out of the waves together.

Things to Consider

How will you make her (yourself) seem middle-aged? _____

_____

_____

How will you make her (yourself) look as if she is carrying a baby and has two other children with her? _____

_____

_____

How will you let the audience know where she is and what she is doing?

_____

_____

_____

How will you express her attitude? _____

_____

_____

_____

Segment Five—Lesson Two *(cont.)*

Acting

Character #7

Your task in this activity is to portray the character described below so that your audience (your classmates) will know as much as possible about him or her. You cannot speak in this exercise, and you will not have the help of costumes or makeup, so you must achieve your effect solely with the bodily/kinesthetic elements of acting.

Do not show your character description to anyone.

Character Description

This character is a little girl. She is hungry, and she is upset because she had a terrible day at school. She can hardly wait to get home. When she gets there, the house is empty.

Things to Consider

How will you make her (yourself) seem like a little girl? _____

_____

_____

How will you get across the idea that she is hungry?_____

_____

_____

How will you express her upset feelings? _____

_____

_____

How will you let the audience know that the house is empty? _____

_____

_____

Segment Five—Lesson Two *(cont.)*

Acting

Character #8

Your task in this activity is to portray the character described below so that your audience (your classmates) will know as much as possible about him or her. You cannot speak in this exercise, and you will not have the help of costumes or makeup, so you must achieve your effect solely with the bodily/kinesthetic elements of acting.

Do not show your character description to anyone.

Character Description

This character is a young girl. She has just received an invitation to a party, and she is very excited. She is looking for her best friend because she wants to share her happiness.

Things to Consider

How will you make her (yourself) seem like a young girl? _____

_____

_____

How will you show that she has just received an invitation? _____

_____

_____

How will you express her excitement? _____

_____

_____

How will you let the audience know that she is looking for her best friend?

_____

_____

_____

_____

Segment Five—Lesson Two *(cont.)*

Acting

Acting Evaluation

Name _____

Name of Performer_____

1. Is the character a man or a woman?

   _____

2. What is the character's age?

   _____

3. Where does the action take place?

   _____

4. What is the character doing?

   _____

5. What is the character's attitude?

   _____

6. What did you like best about this performance?

   _____

   _____

   _____

Segment Five—Lesson Two *(cont.)*

Acting

Translating the Experience

Think about the experience you just had. It was a bodily/kinesthetic experience because you were using your body to portray a character.

Think about your reaction to the experience. Decide how you could translate your reaction by expressing it through another one of the intelligences. Do not use the bodily/kinesthetic intelligence.

Which intelligence will you use to translate your experience?

_____

What materials, if any, will you need?

_____   _____

_____   _____

_____   _____

Will you need time to prepare your translation? How much?

_____

How will you share your translation with the class?

_____

_____

_____

_____

_____

_____

_____

_____

Bodily/ Kinesthetic

Segment Five—Lesson Three

Professional Sports

Purpose: to explain the relationship between the true bodily/kinesthetic experience of the participant and the vicarious bodily/kinesthetic experience of the spectator

Skills: knowledge, comprehension, application, analysis, synthesis, and evaluation

Intelligences: bodily/kinesthetic, visual/spatial, verbal/linguistic, interpersonal, intrapersonal

Materials:

- copies of "Automatic Translation," one for each student

Procedures:

- ◆ Have students review the definition of bodily/kinesthetic intelligence.

- ◆ Give students the definition of "vicarious" (to experience through imagined participation in another's experience).

- ◆ Hold a whole-class discussion of professional sports to check on the level of involvement in your classroom. (If very few students like a sport, watch sports, root for a team, etc., you may want to show some video footage of professional games.)

- ◆ Have students meet in groups to discuss and complete the sheet entitled "Automatic Translation."

- ◆ Use these sheets for discussion during Evaluation and Processing and then place them in the students' folders.

To Simplify:

Allow students to work with aides or parent helpers.

To Expand:

Ask students to find information (pictures, articles, videos, etc.) of their favorite teams and/or players to share with the rest of the class. They could start a sports bulletin board.

Evaluation and Processing:

Allow students to share and discuss their "Automatic Translation" sheets.

Segment Five—Lesson Three *(cont.)*

Professional Sports

Automatic Translation

Athletes who participate in professional sports have a true bodily/kinesthetic experience. One would assume that the spectators would have only a visual/spatial experience while watching a game. However, spectators often have a vicarious bodily/kinesthetic experience. A "vicarious" experience is one that is shared or physically felt by an imagined participation in someone else's experience.

> Have you ever had a vicarious bodily/kinesthetic experience while watching professional sports? Think about your experience. It is as if your body translated a visual/spatial experience into a bodily/kinesthetic one automatically. Use your verbal/linguistic intelligence to write about your reaction to this on the lines below. (If you have never had this experience, write about how you do feel when watching professional sports.)
>
> _____
>
> _____
>
> _____
>
> _____
>
> _____
>
> _____
>
> _____
>
> _____
>
> _____
>
> _____
>
> _____
>
> _____
>
> _____

Bodily/ Kinesthetic

Segment Five—Lesson Four

Using Manipulatives

Purpose: to give students first-hand experience with using manipulatives

Skills: knowledge, comprehension, application, analysis, synthesis, and evaluation

Intelligences: bodily/kinesthetic, verbal/linguistic, interpersonal

Materials:

- supplies of small objects to use for manipulatives
- copies of "Sharing the Experience," one for each student

Procedures:

- ◆ Have students review the definition of bodily/kinesthetic intelligence.
- ◆ Remind students that manipulatives are small objects that can be handled conveniently and used for some purpose. They are often used for counting and for helping students see clearly what is happening during the processes of adding and subtracting. The manipulatives used in a primary classroom might include blocks, buttons, craft sticks, and coins.
- ◆ Pass out the "Sharing the Experience" sheets. This activity will work best if students are in groups (interpersonal). Students will be making packets of manipulatives and designing scripts to teach addition and subtraction concepts, which they can then use when working as cross-age tutors with younger children.
- ◆ You can also use these sheets for discussion during Evaluation and Processing and then place them in the students' folders.

To Simplify:

Allow students to work with aides or parent helpers.

To Expand:

Ask students to make additional packets and scripts during any activity time they have. Also, make one student responsible for a volunteer tutors' sign-up sheet and another responsible for finding out which teachers would like help for their students.

Evaluation and Processing:

Allow students to share and discuss their "Sharing the Experience" sheets and also any experiences that they have in other classrooms as they help younger children to use the packets of manipulatives.

Segment Five—Lesson Four *(cont.)*

Using Manipulatives

A Group Activity—Sharing the Experience

Today you will be working as a group to make math packets for younger children. You will be selecting a math concept that you can demonstrate with manipulatives, creating a script to explain the concept, and choosing the manipulatives that you could use when working as tutors with younger children.

Select a Math Concept

Some things you might choose are single-digit addition or subtraction, double-digit addition or subtraction with or without regrouping, or some special concept you finally understood through the use of manipulatives.

Write a Step-by-Step Script to Use in Explaining the Concept

Work with manipulatives as you practice on each other in your group and write down what you say. Use additional paper, if necessary.

_____

_____

_____

_____

_____

_____

_____

_____

_____

_____

Bodily/ Kinesthetic

Segment Five—Lesson Five

Making Models and Building Things

Purpose: to give students experience in building a model from a kit

Skills: knowledge, comprehension, application, analysis, synthesis, and evaluation

Intelligences: bodily/kinesthetic, verbal/linguistic, interpersonal, intrapersonal

Materials:

- an inexpensive model kit for each group
- copies of "Translating the Experience," one for each student

Procedures:

- ◆ Have students review the definition of bodily/kinesthetic intelligence.
- ◆ Remind students that making models and building things is easy and fun for people with bodily/kinesthetic intelligence. Some of them will have it and some of them will not, but they will never know until they try.
- ◆ Have students divide into groups. Pass out a model kit to each group. They should assign group roles, read the model directions, and try to put it together.
- ◆ Pass out the "Translating the Experience" sheets and have students work individually to complete them.
- ◆ You can also use these sheets for discussion during Evaluation and Processing and then place them in the students' folders.

To Simplify:

Allow students to work with aides or parent helpers.

To Expand:

Encourage students who enjoy model making to bring completed models from home to share with the class.

Evaluation and Processing:

Allow students to share and discuss their "Translating the Experience" sheets, as well as any models they would like to display.

Segment Five—Lesson Five *(cont.)*

Making Models and Building Things

Translating the Experience

Today you have been working in a group to build a model. Did you discover that you have bodily/kinesthetic intelligence, or did you already know? Did you discover that you do not have bodily/kinesthetic intelligence? Was this a frustrating experience? Use your verbal/linguistic intelligence to describe your reaction to this experience on the lines below.

_____

_____

_____

_____

_____

_____

_____

_____

_____

_____

_____

_____

_____

_____

_____

_____

_____

_____

Bodily/ Kinesthetic

Segment Five—Lesson Six

Exercise and Athletics

Purpose: to give students experience in taking part in an athletic game

Skills: knowledge, comprehension, application, analysis, synthesis, and evaluation

Intelligences: bodily/kinesthetic, verbal/linguistic, interpersonal, intrapersonal

Materials:

- bats, balls, gloves, bases (or something to use for bases)
- copies of "Translating the Experience," one for each student

Procedures:

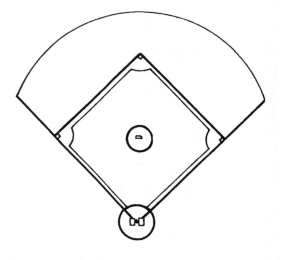

- ◆ Have students review the definition of bodily/kinesthetic intelligence.
- ◆ Divide the class in half at random for teams. Draw straws to see who will be up first.
- ◆ Go out to the playground and play baseball.
- ◆ After the game, pass out the "Translating the Experience" sheets and have students work individually to complete them.
- ◆ You can also use these sheets for discussion during Evaluation and Processing and then place them in the students' folders.

To Simplify:

Allow students to be coached by aides or parent helpers.

To Expand:

Encourage students to continue playing as a class at lunchtime.

Evaluation and Processing:

Allow students to share and discuss their "Translating the Experience" sheets, as well as just discuss the game.

Segment Five—Lesson Six *(cont.)*

Exercise and Athletics

Translating the Experience

Think about the experience you just had. It was a bodily/kinesthetic experience because you used your body to play a game.

Think about your reaction to the experience. Decide how you could translate your reaction by expressing it through another one of the intelligences. Do not express your reaction through your bodily/kinesthetic intelligence.

Which intelligence will you use to translate your experience?

_____

What materials, if any, will you need?

_____   _____

_____   _____

_____   _____

Will you need time to prepare your translation? How much?

_____

How will you share your translation with the class?

_____

_____

_____

_____

_____

_____

_____

Segment Five—Lesson Seven

Gestures and Body Language

Purpose: to give students an experience with body language as it relates to personal space

Skills: knowledge, comprehension, application, analysis, synthesis, and evaluation

Intelligences: Potentially all may be involved.

Materials:

- copies of "Translating the Experience," one for each student

Procedures:

◆ Have students review the definition of bodily/kinesthetic intelligence.

◆ Review and discuss body language with students. (See the "References" section.)

◆ Mark off a space on the classroom floor to serve as an elevator. Have groups of students "enter" the elevator. Have them notice how they stand when there are just a few people on the elevator and how they protect their personal space when the elevator is crowded. What do they look at? What do they do if they bump into another passenger? Discuss.

◆ Pretend that you are all at an amusement park on the last day of summer vacation. The lines are hours long for all of the rides. It is hard to walk down the sidewalks against the flow of people coming the other way. Why are people able to adjust to these conditions? If the "real world" were this crowded, what would probably happen?

◆ After the game, pass out the "Translating the Experience" sheets and have students work individually to complete them.

◆ You can also use these sheets for discussion during Evaluation and Processing and then place them in the students' folders.

To Simplify:

Omit "Translating the Experience."

To Expand:

Encourage students to explore another aspect of body language.

Evaluation and Processing:

Allow students to share and discuss their "Translating the Experience" sheets.

Segment Five—Lesson Seven *(cont.)*

Gestures and Body Language

Translating the Experience

Think about the experience you just had. It was a bodily/kinesthetic experience because you used bodily language to establish your personal space.

Think about your reaction to the experience. Decide how you could translate your reaction by expressing it through another of the intelligences. Do not express your reaction through your bodily/kinesthetic intelligence.

Which intelligence will you use to translate your experience?

_____

What materials, if any, will you need?

_____   _____

_____   _____

_____   _____

Will you need time to prepare your translation? How much?

_____

How will you share your translation with the class?

_____

_____

_____

_____

_____

_____

_____

Bodily/ Kinesthetic

Segment Five—Day Eight

Playing Eye/Hand Coordination Games

Purpose: to give students the opportunity to play games associated with bodily/kinesthetic intelligence

Skills: knowledge, comprehension, application, analysis, synthesis, and evaluation

Intelligences: bodily/kinesthetic, interpersonal, intrapersonal

Materials:

- a number of electronic, interactive games
- copies of "Evaluating the Activity," one for each student
- writing materials

Procedures:

- ◆ Have students review the definition of bodily/kinesthetic intelligence.
- ◆ Ask them to choose an activity and begin.
- ◆ Allow enough time for students to complete an evaluation at the end of the activity.
- ◆ Place evaluation sheets in the students' folders.

To Simplify:

Allow students to work with an aide or helper, if they wish.

To Expand:

Keep games on hand for use during activity times.

Evaluation and Processing:

Share and discuss evaluation sheets.

Segment Five—Lesson Eight *(cont.)*

Playing Eye/Hand Coordination Games

Evaluate the activity in which you participated by responding to the following questions.

1. Which game did you play?

_____

_____

2 If you were playing with a group, will you continue the game later?

_____

_____

3. If you were working alone, will you finish later?

_____

_____

4. Would you ever play this game outside of school? Where? When?

_____

_____

_____

5. Is there another type of game that you prefer? What is it?

_____

_____

_____

_____

Rate this activity from 1 to 10, with10 being best (circle choice):

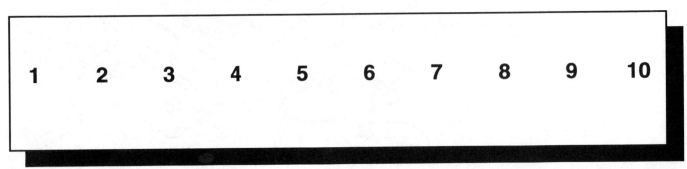

1   2   3   4   5   6   7   8   9   10

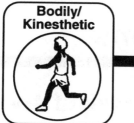

Bodily/ Kinesthetic

Segment Five—Lesson Nine

Sharing Translations

Purpose: to give students the opportunity to share their various translations from bodily/kinesthetic to various other intelligences

Skills: knowledge, comprehension, application, analysis, synthesis, and evaluation

Intelligences: Potentially all may be involved.

Materials:

- individual student folders

Procedures:

◆ Invite students to share the translations from bodily/kinesthetic to any other intelligence they made or planned during this segment.

◆ Allow time for presentations and positive acknowledgements of effort.

To Simplify:

Allow students to work with an aide or helper, if they wish.

To Expand:

Encourage students to use the techniques they learned in this segment on future assignments.

Evaluation and Processing:

This activity is actually an evaluation and processing of the entire segment.

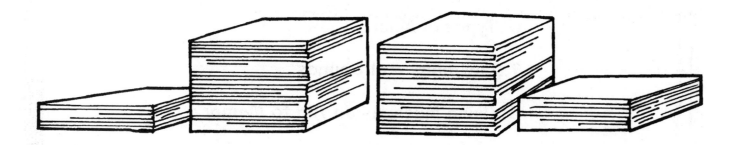

Segment Six—Nine Lessons

From the Middle of March Through the First Week of April

During the sixth segment of this minicurriculum, students will have their fifth experience with archetypal examples of the intelligences, as we consider the musical/rhythmic.

Musical/rhythmic intelligence means thinking in sounds and rhythms—singing on key, remembering and vocally reproducing melodies, moving rhythmically in time to music, and often playing an instrument. People with this kind of intelligence are sensitive to sounds, environmental as well as musical. They often sing, whistle, or hum while engaging in other activities, or make up rhythms and songs to help them remember facts and other information.

The topics in this segment will include suggestions for exposing students to archetypal examples of the musical/rhythmic experience, such as instrumental and vocal music, both classical and modern. The topics will also afford opportunities to look at the elements of music, the different types of music, and at environmental sounds.

The topics selected for this segment are listed below. Brief descriptions and/or explanations follow for your convenience. You may wish to refresh your own familiarity with them. You should, of course, feel free to substitute or add your own favorite topics. If this is "your" intelligence, you will have favorite topics that make this area come alive for you.

1. Instrumental Music

2. Musical Instruments

3. Creating Music Vocally

4. Tone and Its Characteristics

5. Melody, Rhythm, and Tempo

6. Types of Music

7. Environmental Sounds

8. Using Music as an Aid to Memory

9. Sharing Translations

Calendars or Segment Six

Directions: Use the calendars below to plan when you would like to do the nine lessons of this segment. The lessons are listed on the previous page. The highlighted weeks are the time periods which are suggested.

March

M	T	W	T	F
	Segment Six			
	Segment Six			

April

M	T	W	T	F
	Segment Six			

Segment Six

References

1. Instrumental Music

Instrumental music (music played on instruments) is classified by the number of performers who play it:

- Instrumental solos are written to be played by one person.
- Chamber music is written for small combinations of instruments, such as the string quartet (four) and the piano quintet (five).
- Orchestral music is written for an entire orchestra.

Orchestral music:

- rhapsodies (orchestra and soloist)
- concertos (orchestra and soloist)
- symphonies (orchestra alone)

2. Musical Instruments

Musical instruments can be classified according to the way they make sound:

- string
- wind
- percussion

Or they can be classified according to the way they are made:

- stringed
- percussion
- woodwind
- keyboard
- brass
- other (harmonicas and bagpipes, for example)

3. Creating Music Vocally

In vocal music voices are grouped according to their range:

- soprano is the highest woman's voice
- mezzo-soprano sings a little below soprano
- contralto or alto is the lowest woman's voice
- tenor is the highest man's voice
- baritone is the middle range man's voice
- bass is the lowest man's voice

Segment Six *(cont.)*

References *(cont.)*

3. Creating Music Vocally *(cont.)*

Vocal music:

- songs
- choral music
- oratorios
- opera
- light opera and musical comedy

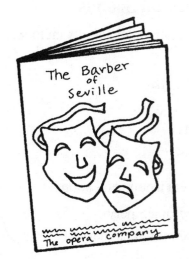

4. Tone and Its Characteristics

The characteristics of tone:

- pitch (high or low)
- duration (long or short)
- quality (played on different instruments)
- intensity (loud or soft)

5. Melody, Rhythm, and Tempo

A melody is a tune—a succession of musical tones played in a fixed pattern of pitches and rhythms.

Rhythm is concerned with:

- duration (long or short)
- accent (strong or weak)

Tempo is the rate of speed at which music is played.

6. Types of Music

The different kinds of music:

- classical
- popular
- hymns
- jazz
- blues
- rock and roll
- folk
- country
- rap

Segment Six *(cont.)*

References *(cont.)*

7. Environmental Sounds

Natural environmental sounds include:

- waves
- waterfalls
- rain
- wind
- birds

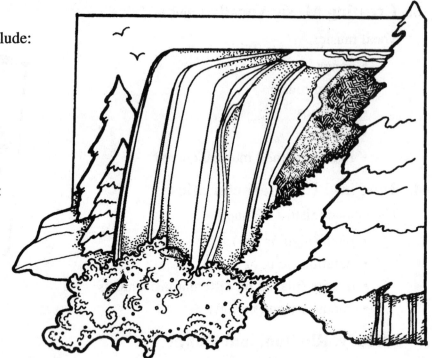

Man-made environmental sounds:

- heavy machinery
- household machinery
- traffic
- trains
- planes
- sirens
- telephones

8. Using Music as an Aid to Memory

Music helps people remember things. You can sing songs about things you need to remember or set the words to a catchy rhythm.

There are also games that help you remember and reproduce musical tones.

9. Sharing Translations

Musical/Rhythmic

Segment Six—Lesson One

Instrumental Music

Purpose: to give students experience with instrumental music

Skills: knowledge, comprehension, application, analysis, synthesis, and evaluation

Intelligences: musical/rhythmic, visual/spatial, verbal/linguistic, interpersonal, intrapersonal

Materials:

Note: Before using any outside audio or video resources, obtain the necessary district permission.

- a recording of Beethoven's *Symphony No. 9 in D minor*
- a copy of the video *I See a Song* (This is the fifth selection in *The Very Hungry Caterpillar and Other Stories* by Eric Carle. Although it is distributed by Disney Videos and advertised as a video for very young children, it is an ageless gem in which a violin solo is translated into designs made of swirling colors.)
- copies of "A Visual/Spatial Translation," one for each student

Procedures:

◆ Have students review the definition of musical/rhythmic intelligence.

◆ Introduce this experience by giving a brief overview of instrumental music. (See the 'References" section.)

◆ Play a recording of Beethoven's *Symphony No. 9 in D minor*, especially the chorus, which contains the popular "Ode To Joy," and allow students to just listen. (If you have another favorite lyrical piece that you think the students would enjoy, feel free to substitute it.)

◆ Then, without any further discussion, play the video of *I See a Song* and ask students to work individually on the sheet entitled "A Visual/Spatial Translation."

◆ Use these sheets for discussion during Evaluation and Processing and then place them in the students' folders.

To Simplify:

Simply listen to the music and watch the video.

To Expand:

Ask students to find other orchestral pieces that they would like to share with the class.

Evaluation and Processing:

Allow students to share and discuss their "A Visual/Spatial Translation" sheets.

Segment Six—Lesson One *(cont.)*

Instrumental Music

A Visual/Spatial Translation

The video you are about to watch is a visual/spatial translation of a musical/rhythmic experience.

Watch the video of *I See a Song*.

Think about the experience you just had. This was the way an artist translated sound into color and design.

Think about your reaction to the experience. Use your verbal/linguistic intelligence to write about your reaction on the lines below.

_____

_____

_____

_____

_____

_____

_____

_____

_____

_____

_____

_____

_____

_____

Segment Six—Lesson Two

Musical Instruments

Purpose: to give students information about musical instruments

Skills: knowledge, comprehension, application, analysis, synthesis, and evaluation

Intelligences: musical/rhythmic, visual/spatial, verbal/linguistic, interpersonal, intrapersonal

Materials:

Note: Before using any outside audio or video resources, obtain the necessary district permission.

- copies of "The Musical Instruments," one set for each student
- a copy of the Disney video *Peter and the Wolf* (This is the Disney version of the classic orchestral piece of the same name written by Sergei Prokofiev, a Russian composer. The animals in the Disney story speak in the voices of several different musical instruments.)
- copies of "A Visual/Spatial Translation," one for each student

Procedures:

- ◆ Have students review the definition of musical/rhythmic intelligence.
- ◆ Pass out sets of "The Musical Instruments."
- ◆ Introduce this experience by giving a brief overview of the musical instruments. (See Suggested References on page 226.)
- ◆ Then, without any further discussion, play the video of *Peter and the Wolf* and ask students to work individually on the sheet entitled "A Visual/Spatial Translation."
- ◆ Use these sheets for discussion during Evaluation and Processing and then place them in the students' folders.

To Simplify:

Simply listen to the music and watch the video.

To Expand:

Ask the students to find another orchestral piece and try to list the instruments they hear in it.

Evaluation and Processing:

Allow students to share and discuss their "A Visual/Spatial Translation" sheets.

Segment Six—Lesson Two *(cont.)*

Musical Instruments

Members of the String Family

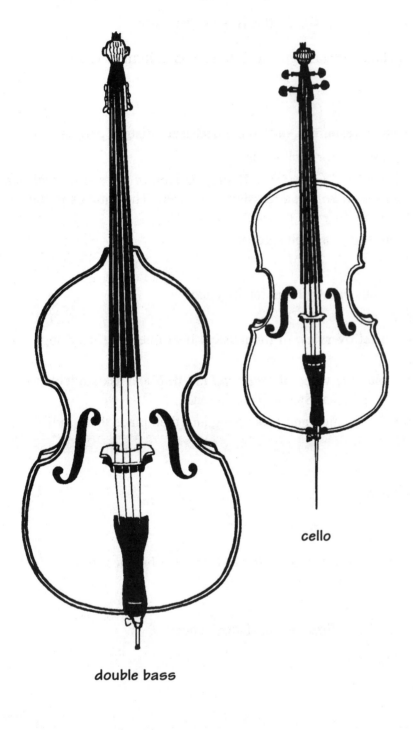

double bass

cello

viola   violin

harp

Segment Six—Lesson Two (cont.)

Musical Instruments

Members of the Brass Family

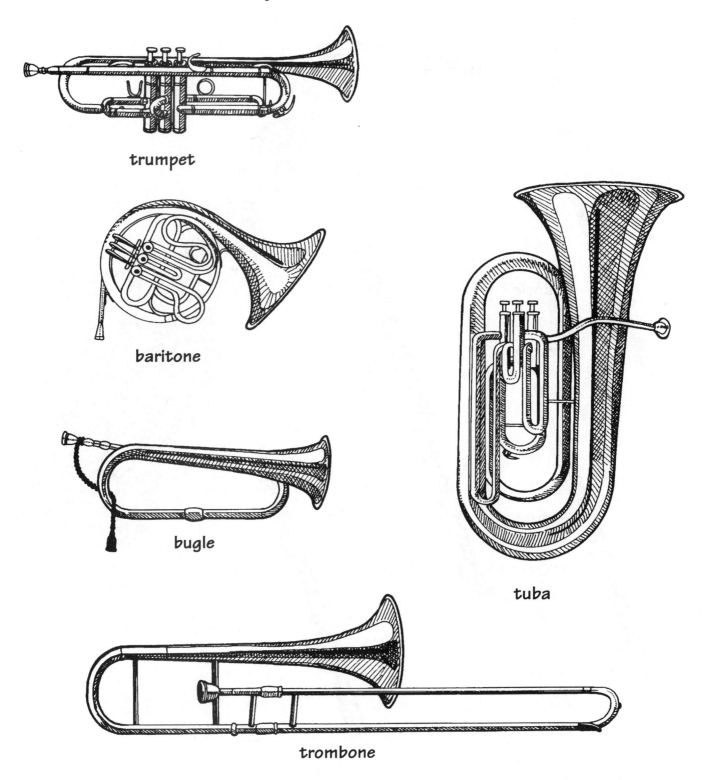

trumpet

baritone

bugle

tuba

trombone

Segment Six—Lesson Two *(cont.)*

Musical Instruments

Members of the Woodwind Family

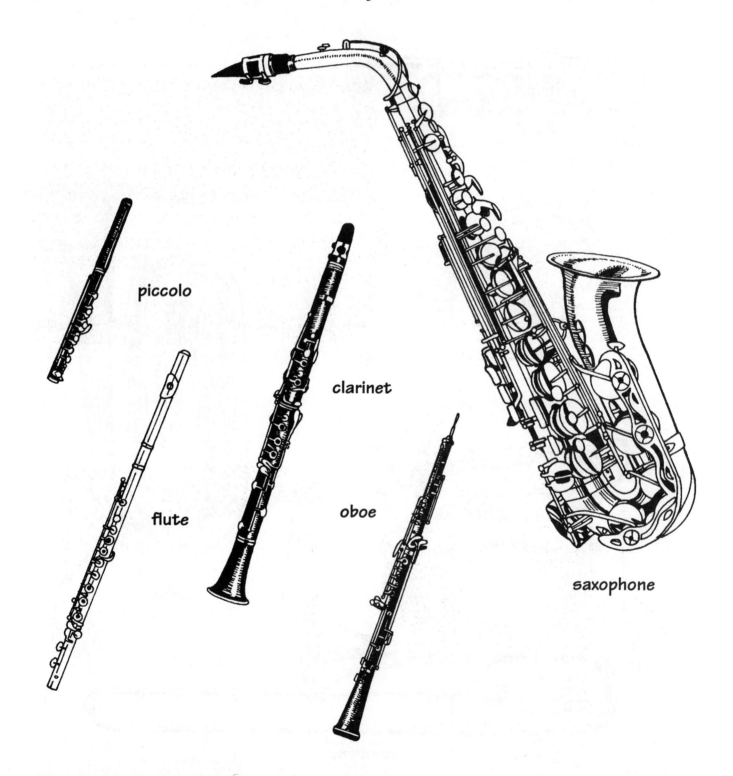

piccolo

flute

clarinet

oboe

saxophone

Segment Six—Lesson Two *(cont.)*

Musical Instruments

Members of the Percussion Family

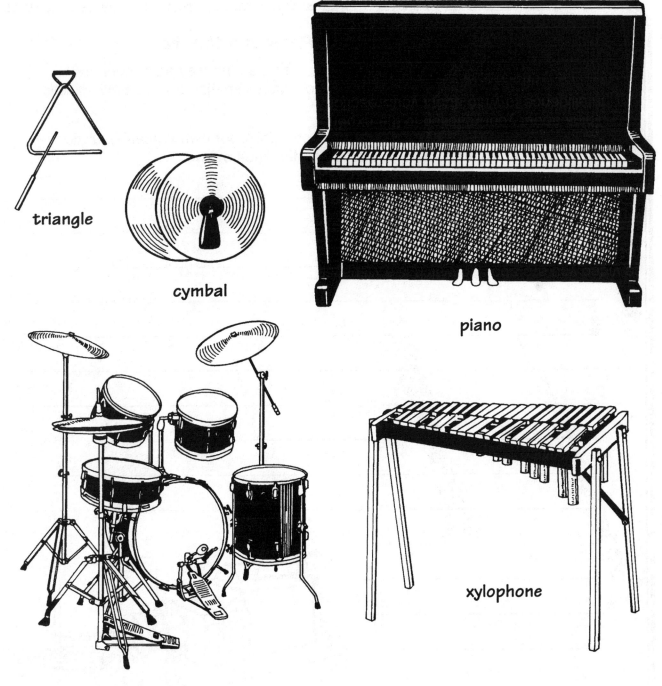

triangle

cymbal

piano

drums

xylophone

Segment Six—Lesson Two *(cont.)*

Musical Instruments

A Visual/Spatial Translation

The video you are about to watch is a visual/spatial translation of a musical/rhythmic experience.

Watch the video of *Peter and the Wolf.*

Think about the experience you just had. This was the way animators and storytellers translated musical sounds into a visual/spatial (and verbal/linguistic) experience.

Think about your reaction to the experience. Use your own verbal/linguistic intelligence to write about your reaction on the lines below.

_____

_____

_____

_____

_____

_____

_____

_____

_____

_____

_____

Musical/ Rhythmic

Segment Six—Lesson Three

Creating Music Vocally

Purpose: to give students information about vocal music as it is used in musicals

Skills: knowledge, comprehension, application, analysis, synthesis, and evaluation

Intelligences: Potentially all may be involved.

Materials:

- a recording of a fairly recent well-known musical, such as *Cats* or *Evita,* or an older one, such as *The Music Man* (If you have a favorite musical, use it instead.)

- copies of "Translating the Experience," one for each student

Procedures:

◆ Have students review the definition of musical/rhythmic intelligence.

◆ Introduce this experience by giving a brief overview of vocal music. (See the "References" section.)

◆ Then, without any further discussion, play the recording of the musical you selected and ask students to work individually on the sheet entitled "Translating the Experience."

◆ Use these sheets for discussion during Evaluation and Processing and then place them in the students' folders.

To Simplify:
Simply listen to the music.

To Expand:
Ask students to find other musicals that they would like to share with the class.

Evaluation and Processing:
Allow students to share and discuss their sheets entitled "Translating the Experience."

Segment Six—Lesson Three *(cont.)*

Creating Music Vocally

Translating the Experience

Think about the experience you just had. It was a musical/rhythmic experience. You listened to the way in which voices were used to create music.

Think about your reaction to the experience. Decide how you could translate your reaction by expressing it through another one of the intelligences. Do not express your reaction through your musical/rhythmic intelligence!

Which intelligence will you use to translate your experience?

_____

What materials, if any, will you need?

_____   _____

_____   _____

_____   _____

Will you need time to prepare your translation? How much?

_____

How will you share your translation with the class?

_____

_____

_____

_____

_____

_____

_____

Now Playing "Eldorado"

Musical/ Rhythmic

Segment Six—Lesson Four

Tone and Its Characteristics

Purpose: to give students an experience with tone and its characteristics

Skills: knowledge, comprehension, application, analysis, synthesis, and evaluation

Intelligences: musical/rhythmic, bodily/kinesthetic, verbal/linguistic, interpersonal, intrapersonal

Materials:

- a selection of easy-to-play "school type" musical instruments, such as autoharps, xylophones, and a piano (if you have access to one)
- copies of "Translating the Experience," one for each student

Procedures:

◆ Have students review the definition of musical/rhythmic intelligence.

◆ Introduce this experience by giving a brief overview of tone and its characteristics. (See the "References" section.)

◆ Give students as much time as possible to use the musical instruments to investigate the characteristic of tone. Write important, tone-related words on the board.

◆ The characteristics of tone:
  - pitch (high or low)
  - duration (long or short)
  - quality (played on different instruments)
  - intensity (loud or soft)

◆ Then, without any further discussion, ask students to work individually on the sheet entitled "Translating the Experience."

◆ Use thse sheets entitled for discussion during Evaluation and Processing and then place them in the students' folders.

To Simplify:

Allow students to work with aides or parent helpers.

To Expand:

Ask students to listen to music at home, making notes about the examples they find of the characteristics of tone.

Evaluation and Processing:

Allow students to share and discuss their sheets entitled "Translating the Experience."

Segment Six—Lesson Four *(cont.)*

Tone and Its Characteristics

Translating the Experience

Think about the experience you just had. It was a musical/rhythmic experience. You experimented with the characteristics of tone by using different musical instruments.

Think about your reaction to the experience. Use your verbal/linguistic intelligence to write about your reaction on the lines below.

_____

_____

_____

_____

_____

_____

_____

_____

_____

_____

_____

_____

_____

_____

_____

_____

_____

_____

Musical/ Rhythmic

Segment Six—Lesson Five

Melody, Rhythm, and Tempo

Purpose: to give students a first-hand experience with rhythm

Skills: knowledge, comprehension, application, analysis, synthesis, and evaluation

Intelligences: musical/rhythmic, bodily/kinesthetic, verbal/linguistic, interpersonal, intrapersonal

Materials:

- recordings of several pieces of music with strong distinctive beats, such as a waltz (one-two-three, one-two-three) and a march (one-two-one-two)

- copies of "Translating the Experience," one for each student

Procedures:

◆ Have students review the definition of musical/rhythmic intelligence.

◆ Introduce this experience by giving a brief overview of melody, rhythm, and tempo. (See the "References" section.)

◆ Give students as much time as possible to beat or clap the rhythms of the pieces you play.

◆ Then, without any further discussion, ask students to work individually on the sheet entitled "Translating the Experience."

◆ Use these sheets for discussion during Evaluation and Processing and then place them in the students' folders.

To Simplify:

Allow students to work with aides or parent helpers.

To Expand:

Ask students to listen to music at home and make notes about the examples of rhythm they find.

Evaluation and Processing:

Allow students to share and discuss their sheets entitled "Translating the Experience."

Segment Six—Lesson Five *(cont.)*

Melody, Rhythm, and Tempo

Translating the Experience

Think about the experience you just had. It was a musical/rhythmic experience. You experimented with the characteristics of rhythm as illustrated by different pieces of music.

Think about your reaction to the experience. Use your verbal/linguistic intelligence to write about your reaction on the lines below.

_____

_____

_____

_____

_____

_____

_____

_____

_____

_____

_____

_____

_____

_____

_____

Musical/ Rhythmic

Segment Six—Lesson Six

Types of Music

Purpose: to give students information about many of the different kinds of music

Skills: knowledge, comprehension, application, analysis, synthesis, and evaluation

Intelligences: musical/rhythmic, verbal/linguistic, interpersonal, intrapersonal

Materials:

- copies of "Keeping Track of Information," one for each student

- copies of "Translating the Experience," one for each student

Procedures:

◆ Have students review the definition of musical/rhythmic intelligence.

◆ Introduce this experience by writing the names of these different kinds of music on the chalkboard: classical, popular, hymns, jazz, blues, rock and roll, folk, country, rap.

◆ Pass out "Keeping Track of Information" and have the students work together in groups to fill it in. They can consult reference books if they need to.

◆ Then, without any further discussion, ask the students to work individually on the sheet entitled "Translating the Experience."

◆ Use these sheets for discussion during Evaluation and Processing and then place them in the students' folders.

To Simplify:

Allow your students to work with aides or parent helpers.

To Expand:

Ask your students to finish the form entitled "Keeping Track of Information" at home by getting additional information from family members or friends.

Evaluation and Processing:

Allow the students to share and discuss their sheets entitled "Translating the Experience."

Segment Six—Lesson Six *(cont.)*

Types of Music

Keeping Track of Information

With your group, think of examples for each of the following types of music and fill in your chart. You may use reference books for help.

Type of Music	Example	Composer	Artist
Classical			
Popular			
Hymns			
Jazz			
Blues			
Rock and Roll			
Folk			
Country			
Rap			

Segment Six—Lesson Six *(cont.)*

Types of Music

Translating the Experience

Think about the experience you just had. It was not a musical/rhythmic experience. What kind of an experience was it? _____

Decide how you could translate it into a musical experience.

_____

What materials, if any, will you need?

_____   _____

_____   _____

_____   _____

Will you need time to prepare your translation? How much?

_____

How will you share your translation with the class?

_____

_____

_____

_____

_____

_____

_____

_____

_____

_____

Musical/ Rhythmic

Segment Six—Lesson Seven

Environmental Sounds

Purpose: to make students aware of the sounds in their environment

Skills: knowledge, comprehension, application, analysis, synthesis, and evaluation

Intelligences: Potentially all may be involved.

Materials:

- a recording of environmental sounds (Get one with a variety of types.)

- copies of "Translating the Experience," one for each student

Procedures:

- ◆ Have students review the definition of musical/rhythmic intelligence.

- ◆ Introduce this experience by discussing the two classes of environmental sounds and asking the students for input. (See the "References" section.)

- ◆ Play the recording of environmental sounds. Ask students to identify them and decide which ones are pleasant and which ones cause stress.

- ◆ Then, without any further discussion, ask students to work individually on the sheet entitled "Translating the Experience."

- ◆ Use the sheets for discussion during Evaluation and Processing and then place them in the students' folders.

To Simplify:

Allow students to work with aides or parent helpers.

To Expand:

Ask students to brainstorm for ideas to control unpleasant noises in the environment.

Evaluation and Processing:

Allow students to share and discuss their sheets entitled "Translating the Experience."

Segment Six—Lesson Seven *(cont.)*

Environmental Sounds

Translating the Experience

Think about the experience you just had. It was a musical/rhythmic experience. You listened to some of the sounds that occur in the environment.

Think about your reaction to the experience. Decide how you could translate your reaction by expressing it through another one of the intelligences. Do not express your reaction through your musical/rhythmic intelligence!

Which intelligence will you use to translate your experience?

_____

What materials, if any, will you need?

_____   _____

_____   _____

_____   _____

Will you need time to prepare your translation? How much?

_____

How will you share your translation with the class?

_____

_____

_____

_____

_____

_____

_____

Segment Six—Lesson Eight

Using Music as an Aid to Memory

Purpose: to give students an experience in using musical/rhythmic intelligence as an aid to memory

Skills: knowledge, comprehension, application, analysis, synthesis, and evaluation

Intelligences: musical/rhythmic, verbal/linguistic, interpersonal, intrapersonal

Materials:

- copies of "Musical Memory Aids," one for each student

- scratch paper

Procedures:

- ◆ Have students review the definition of musical/rhythmic intelligence.

- ◆ Introduce this experience by discussing the fact that music can be used as an aid to memory. (See the "References" section.)

- ◆ Tell the students that they will be creating their own musical memory aids.

- ◆ Have the students work in groups to create their own musical memory aids with the assistance of the sheet entitled "Musical Memory Aids."

- ◆ Use these sheets for discussion during Evaluation and Processing and then place them in the students' folders.

To Simplify:

Allow the students to work with aides or parent helpers.

To Expand:

Encourage your students to make more than one musical memory aid and share the results with the class.

Evaluation and Processing:

Allow the students to share and discuss their sheets entitled "Musical Memory Aids."

Segment Six—Lesson Eight (cont.)

Using Music as an Aid to Memory

Name _____

Musical Memory Aids

What do you want to be able to remember? _____

_____

_____

Would you rather create a song or a rap-type rhythm? _____

_____

Try writing your ideas down on scratch paper. Copy the completed product below. Be ready to share.

_____

_____

_____

_____

_____

_____

_____

_____

_____

_____

_____

_____

Musical/ Rhythmic

Segment Six—Lesson Nine

Sharing Translations

Purpose: to give students the opportunity to share their various translations from musical/rhythmic to various other intelligences

Skills: knowledge, comprehension, application, analysis, synthesis, and evaluation

Intelligences: Potentially all may be involved.

Materials:

- individual student folders

Procedures:

◆ Invite students to share the translations from musical/rhythmic to any other intelligence they made or planned during this segment.

◆ Allow time for presentations and positive acknowledgements of effort.

To Simplify:

Allow the students to work with an aide or helper, if they wish.

To Expand:

Encourage the students to use the techniques they learned in this segment on future assignments.

Evaluation and Processing:

This activity is actually an evaluation and processing of the entire segment.

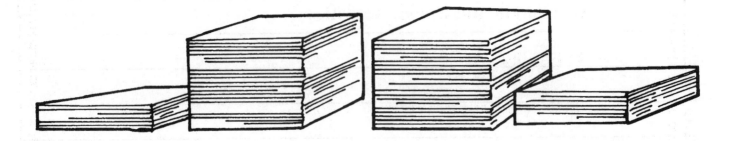

Segment Seven—Nine Lessons

From the Middle of April Through the First Week of May

During the seventh segment of this minicurriculum, students will have their sixth experience with archetypal examples of the intelligences, as we consider the interpersonal.

Interpersonal means tending to turn outward and connect with other people—enjoying family, friends, and social activities of all kinds. People with this kind of intelligence enjoy working in groups, learn while interacting and cooperating, and are reluctant to be alone. Usually empathetic, they often serve as mediators in case of disputes, both in school situations and at home. Conversation is a form of recreation to people with interpersonal intelligence.

The topics in this segment will include suggestions for exposing students to archetypal examples of interpersonal intelligence, for example, group work of various kinds, experiences with empathy and reaching consensus, conflict resolution, and social activities with friends and family.

The topics selected for this segment are listed below. Brief descriptions and/or explanations follow for your convenience. You may wish to refresh your own familiarity with them. You should, of course, feel free to substitute or add your own favorite topics. If this is "your" intelligence, you will have favorite topics that make this area come alive for you.

1. **Group Work**

2. **Teams**

3. **Reaching Consensus/Conflict Resolution/Empathy**

4. **School and Student Body Responsibility**

5. **Public Speaking**

6. **Friends and Social Activities**

7. **Family**

8. **Conversation/Letter Writing**

9. **Sharing Translations and Activity Sheets**

Calendars for Segment Seven

Directions: Use the calendars below to plan when you would like to do the nine lessons of this segment. The lessons are listed on the previous page. The highlighted weeks are the time periods which are suggested.

April

M	T	W	T	F
		Segment Seven		
		Segment Seven		

May

M	T	W	T	F
		Segment Seven		

Segment Seven

References

1. Group Work

Cooperative group work is not necessarily a skill that comes naturally to people unless their dominant intelligence is interpersonal. It is, however, a skill that is becoming more and more important both in school and in the workplace.

Cooperative groups, in order to be effective, should have certain characteristics:

- mutual trust among the members of the group
- acceptance of individual responsibility for the group's success
- ability of group members to work together rather than compete
- ability of group members to recognize and appreciate differences

2. Teams

A team is a very special kind of group. It is made up of people who are working together for a special purpose. A team often makes up one side in a contest or competition. The people on a team are often held together not only by wanting to cooperate with each other but also by wanting to win or to beat another team.

The special quality of a team is shown by some of the words we use:

- a teammate—a fellow player on a team
- a team player—a person who puts the team first before his or her own interests
- team spirit—the special way people on a team feel about their group
- teamwork—the kind of work that results when the team is more important than the individual members

3. Reaching Consensus/Conflict Resolution/Empathy

Consensus means general agreement. Reaching consensus means getting to a place where everyone agrees.

Conflict is a sharp disagreement. Conflict resolution is the process of finding out why people do not agree and then taking steps to solve the problem.

Empathy is the ability to share in another person's thoughts, feelings, and emotions. If someone said to you, "Try to put yourself in my place," that person would be asking you to have empathy. People who are good at reaching consensus and at conflict resolution usually have empathy.

Segment Seven (cont.)

References (cont.)

4. School and Student Body Responsibility

Very often people with interpersonal intelligence get involved with school and student body responsibilities. They love being part of things, knowing what is going on, and helping to run an organization.

5. Public Speaking

Public speaking is one of those things that almost everyone has to do at some time or another. Several surveys have indicated that people, in general, fear speaking in public more than they fear dying!

It is also known that the more people speak in public (even if they are afraid) the easier it gets. People join organizations such as Toastmasters in order to give themselves a chance to practice their public speaking skills.

The speeches themselves can be divided into three main categories: speeches that inform, speeches that persuade, and speeches that entertain. These categories can, of course, overlap. If a speech informs and entertains, it might be more persuasive, depending on the subject matter.

When a speaker knows the kind of speech he or she plans to give, it is then time to think about the audience. Experts want to know things that beginners would not understand. A speech about making pancakes, for example, would be very different if addressed to an audience of chefs than if addressed to a group of boys or girls who were preparing for their first camp-out. It also helps to know if the audience is for or against the subject you plan to talk about.

6. Friends and Social Activities

Many people have lots of friends and so many social activities that they cannot get to all of them. Other people have trouble making friends and are always wishing that they had something to do.

If you want to make friends more easily, here are some things you can do:

- smile more
- say "hello" first
- act interested in other people
- invite someone to do something with you
- join a club
- take up a sport
- join a team

Segment Seven *(cont.)*

References *(cont.)*

7. Family

Families are very important, but they are not all the same. Only some people come from the "standard" family of two parents and two children. Families are groups of people who care a lot about each other, are usually related in some way, and very often live together. Examples of families who do not live together are people with grandparents who live at a distance, parents who are divorced, or older brothers and sisters who are off at college or working far away.

People with strong interpersonal intelligence are often close to their families, but not always. Sometimes people use all their social skills on outsiders. It is a good idea for family members to be just as nice to each other as they are to their friends.

8. Conversation/Letter Writing

Conversation is casual talk or the verbal exchange of ideas and opinions. It is relaxing and recreational to the person with strong interpersonal skills.

Letter writing is much like a written conversation. Some people write their letters on computer E-mail. Letter writing does not demand as much in the way of interpersonal skills as does conversation because there is no immediate give-and-take. One person can say everything he or she wants to say, and then the other person can take an uninterrupted turn.

9. Sharing Translations and Activity Sheets

Interpersonal

Segment Seven—Lesson One

Group Work

Purpose: to give students experience in setting up the rules and environment for group work

Skills: knowledge, comprehension, application, analysis, synthesis, and evaluation

Intelligences: interpersonal, verbal/linguistic

Materials:

- copies of "Making It Work," one for each student

Procedures:

◆ Have students review the definition of interpersonal intelligence.

◆ Introduce this experience by giving a brief overview of group work. (See the "References" section.)

◆ Based on the brief overview of group work and on any cooperative group work that the students have done, ask them to come up with a plan to ensure that all the requirements for group work can be met.

◆ Have the students work in groups and use the sheet called "Making It Work" to record their ideas.

◆ Use these sheets for discussion during Evaluation and Processing and then place them in the students' folders.

To Simplify:

Have students work with aides or parent volunteers.

To Expand:

Ask students to discuss and/or write about how they feel about cooperative learning groups in school. Are they comfortable with this way of learning? If they have any concerns, would these concerns be helped by implementing any of the ideas that they came up with for "Making It Work"?

Evaluation and Processing:

Encourage students to compare and discuss the ideas they recorded on the sheets entitled "Making It Work." Have them choose one or more of these ideas that they would like to help you implement in your classroom.

Segment Seven—Lesson One (cont.)

Group Work

Making It Happen

These are the characteristics cooperative groups should have:

- mutual trust among the members of the group
- acceptance of individual responsibility for the group's success
- ability of group members to work together rather than compete
- ability of group members to recognize and appreciate differences

What could be done to make sure a cooperative group would have these characteristics? Write your ideas below. If you need more room, use another sheet of paper.

1. mutual trust among the members of the group

    _____

    _____

    _____

    _____

2. acceptance of individual responsibility for the group's success

    _____

    _____

    _____

    _____

3. ability of group members to work together rather than compete

    _____

    _____

    _____

    _____

4. ability of group members to recognize and appreciate differences

    _____

    _____

    _____

Interpersonal

Segment Seven—Lesson Two

Teams

Purpose: to give students the opportunity to analyze their feelings about teams

Skills: knowledge, comprehension, application, analysis, synthesis, and evaluation

Intelligences: interpersonal, verbal/linguistic, intrapersonal

Materials:

- copies of "Teams Are . . . ," one for each student

Procedures:

◆ Have students review the definition of interpersonal intelligence.

◆ Introduce this experience by giving a brief overview of teams. (See the "References" section.)

◆ Based on the brief overview of teams and on any team experience that the students may have had, ask them to work individually to complete "Teams Are . . .".

◆ Use these sheets for discussion during Evaluation and Processing and then place them in the students' folders.

To Simplify:

Have students work with aides or parent volunteers.

To Expand:

Ask students to work in a group to further discuss how they feel about teams. What do they like best? What would they change if they could?

Evaluation and Processing:

Encourage students to compare and discuss their remarks on "Teams Are . . ." Ask for volunteers to read their pages aloud.

Segment Seven—Lesson Two *(cont.)*

Teams

Teams Are . . .

Think about teams and the information your teacher just gave you about them and any experiences you yourself have had. How do you feel about being on a team? What does it mean when people say they put their teams first? Do you think people should put their teams first? How do you feel about competing with another team? How do you feel about winning or losing?

Being on a team is a special kind of interpersonal experience. Use your intrapersonal and verbal/linguistic intelligences to think and write about teams on the lines below.

_____

_____

_____

_____

_____

_____

_____

_____

_____

_____

_____

_____

_____

Interpersonal

Segment Seven—Lesson Three

Reaching Consensus/Conflict Resolution/Empathy

Purpose: to give students the opportunity to consider and share their understanding of empathy

Skills: knowledge, comprehension, application, analysis, synthesis, and evaluation

Intelligences: interpersonal, verbal/linguistic, intrapersonal

Materials:

- copies of "The Most Uncomfortable Emotion," one for each student

Procedures:

◆ Have students review the definition of interpersonal intelligence.

◆ Introduce this experience by giving a brief overview of the topic. (See the "References" section.)

◆ Ask students to consider the definition of empathy for a few minutes to determine if they have ever experienced it. Write these questions on the board: (Students will also find them on the sheet entitled "The Most Uncomfortable Emotion.")

    – What is sympathy? How is it different from empathy?
    – Empathy has been called the most uncomfortable human emotion. What do you suppose that means?
    – Is it possible to be happy when feeling empathy?

◆ Encourage students to share their experiences with empathy.

◆ Then have students work individually to complete the sheet entitled "The Most Uncomfortable Emotion."

◆ Use these sheets for discussion during Evaluation and Processing and then place them in the students' folders.

To Simplify:

Have students work with aides or parent volunteers.

To Expand:

Ask students to express the meaning of empathy through their visual/spatial intelligence.

Evaluation and Processing:

Encourage students to compare and discuss their remarks on "The Most Uncomfortable Emotion."

Segment Seven—Lesson Three *(cont.)*

Reaching Consensus/Conflict Resolution/Empathy

The Most Uncomfortable Emotion

On the lines below, write about an experience you have had with empathy. You can use these questions to help you get started:

- What is *sympathy*? How is it different from *empathy*?
- Empathy has been called the most uncomfortable human emotion. What do you suppose that means?
- Is it possible to be happy when feeling empathy?

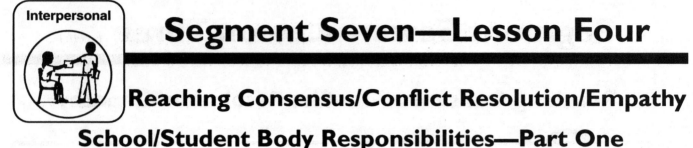

Interpersonal

Segment Seven—Lesson Four

Reaching Consensus/Conflict Resolution/Empathy

School/Student Body Responsibilities—Part One

Purpose: to give students the opportunity to consider running for school office

Skills: knowledge, comprehension, application, analysis, synthesis, and evaluation

Intelligences: interpersonal, verbal/linguistic, intrapersonal

Materials:

- copies of "Running for Office," one for each student

Procedures:

◆ Have students review the definition of interpersonal intelligence.

◆ Introduce this experience by giving a brief overview of the topic. (See the "References" section.)

◆ Announce a classroom election. (This almost has to be real!) Say that everyone is eligible, everyone must pick an office to run for, and everyone must prepare a campaign speech.

◆ Discuss the responsibilities involved in each office. (The positions are president, vice-president, secretary, and treasurer. You can decide what the responsibilities of each position will be according to the needs of your classroom.)

◆ Pass out "Running for Office." Go over it with students and let them get started.

◆ When everyone is finished, place completed sheets in the students' folders to be saved for the next activity, public speaking.

To Simplify:

This part of the two-part activity is standard for everyone. (See pages 264–265 for part two.)

To Expand:

This part of the two-part activity is standard for everyone.

Evaluation and Processing:

The evaluation and processing of this two-part activity will take part on the second day.

Segment Seven—Lesson Four *(cont.)*

Reaching Consensus/Conflict Resolution/Empathy

Name _____

Running for Office

1. Circle the office you want to run for:

| President | Vice President | Secretary | Treasurer |

2. Write your campaign speech.

- Tell why you are the right person for the office.
- Tell what you will do if you are elected.

_____

_____

_____

_____

_____

_____

_____

_____

_____

_____

_____

_____

_____

_____

_____

Interpersonal

Segment Seven—Lesson Five

Public Speaking—Part Two

Purpose: to give students the experience of making a campaign speech

Skills: knowledge, comprehension, application, analysis, synthesis, and evaluation

Intelligences: interpersonal, verbal/linguistic, bodily/kinesthetic

Materials:

- copies of "Classroom Ballots," one for each student

Procedures:

◆ Have students review the definition of interpersonal intelligence.

◆ Devote the entire time period to campaign speeches.

◆ When all the speeches have been given, pass out "Classroom Ballots" and have students vote.

◆ When everyone is finished, collect the ballots and count them.

To Simplify:

This part of the two-part activity is standard for everyone. (See pages 262–263 for part one.)

To Expand:

This part of the two-part activity is standard for everyone.

Evaluation and Processing:

Encourage students to discuss the experience. Was it hard? Was it fun? If you were going to do it again, would you do anything differently?

Segment Seven—Lesson Five *(cont.)*

Public Speaking

Classroom Ballots

Write in the name of the person you are voting for after the name of the office.

Vote only once for each office.

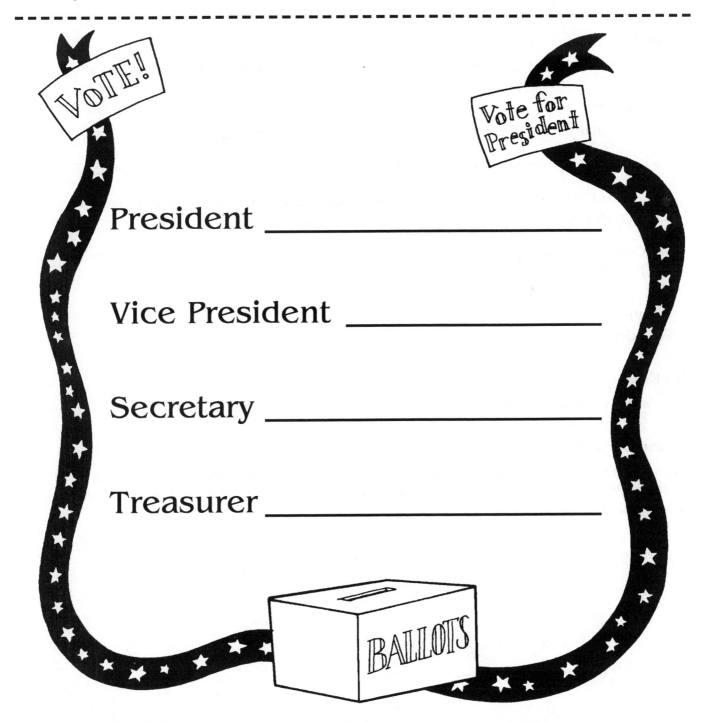

President _____

Vice President _____

Secretary _____

Treasurer _____

Interpersonal

Segment Seven—Lesson Six

Friends and Social Activities

Purpose: to give students information about making and keeping friends

Skills: knowledge, comprehension, application, analysis, synthesis, and evaluation

Intelligences: interpersonal, verbal/linguistic, intrapersonal

Materials:

- copies of "An Intrapersonal Look at an Interpersonal Experience," one for each student

Procedures:

- ◆ Have students review the definition of interpersonal intelligence.

- ◆ Introduce this experience by giving a brief overview of the topic. (See the "References" section.)

- ◆ Pass out "An Intrapersonal Look at an Interpersonal Experience" and have students work on it individually.

- ◆ Give students the option to take this paper home for private keeping or have them put it in their folders.

To Simplify:

This activity is standard for everyone.

To Expand:

This activity is standard for everyone.

Evaluation and Processing:

Ask volunteers to share. Many students will not want to. You might want to try discussing it in the abstract: Was this a valuable activity? Would you rather use your interpersonal or intrapersonal intelligence?

Segment Seven—Lesson Six *(cont.)*

Friends and Social Activities

An Intrapersonal Look at an Interpersonal Experience

Take an intrapersonal look at your interpersonal relationships by answering the questions below:

No one else will look at your answers.

There are no right or wrong answers—just things to think about.

1. Do you have as many friends as you want to have?

   _____

2. Do you like people in general?

   _____

3. Do you feel as if people like you? Why?

   _____

   _____

   _____

4. Do you feel as if people do not like you? Why?

   _____

   _____

   _____

5. What is the one thing about you that you feel is the most *attractive* to other people?

   _____

6. What is the thing about you that you feel is the most *unattractive* to other people?

   _____

7. If you could magically change one thing about yourself, what would it be?

   _____

   _____

Interpersonal

Segment Seven—Lesson Seven

Families

Purpose: to initiate an interpersonal activity involving families

Skills: knowledge, comprehension, application, analysis, synthesis, and evaluation

Intelligences: interpersonal, verbal/linguistic, intrapersonal

Materials:

- copies of "A Family Party," one for each student

Procedures:

- ◆ Have students review the definition of interpersonal intelligence.

- ◆ Introduce this experience by giving a brief overview of the topic. (See the "References" section.)

- ◆ Ask students: Do you have enough time to spend having fun with your family? When was the last time you all did something together? Have you ever given a party for your family?

- ◆ Suggest a family party at school for which they can do all the planning. They can plan such things as when, where, what foods, how to pay for it, etc.

- ◆ Pass out "A Family Party" and have students work on it in groups.

- ◆ Use these completed sheets for discussion during Evaluation and Processing and then place them in the students' folders.

To Simplify:

This activity is standard for everyone.

To Expand:

This activity is standard for everyone.

Evaluation and Processing:

Ask your recently elected class secretary to make a composite copy of the actvity sheets. As soon as you see if the ideas are workable, have your class officers take over the party project. Make sure they know you will help if needed but try to let them do it all.

Segment Seven—Lesson Seven *(cont.)*

Families

A Family Party

Name _____

Write your ideas and suggestions below.

When?_____

Where? _____

What food? _____

_____

_____

How can we pay for it? _____

_____

In the space provided, write about other ideas or suggestions you may have.

_____

_____

_____

_____

_____

_____

_____

_____

_____

_____

_____

_____

Interpersonal

Segment Seven—Lesson Eight

Conversation/Letter Writing

Purpose: to give students a first-hand experience in letter writing

Skills: knowledge, comprehension, application, analysis, synthesis, and evaluation

Intelligences: interpersonal, verbal/linguistic, intrapersonal

Materials:

- copies of "Writing a Letter," one for each student

Procedures:

◆ Have students review the definition of interpersonal intelligence.

◆ Introduce this experience by giving a brief overview of the topic. (See the "References" section.)

◆ Put everyone's name in a hat and have students draw the name of the classmate to whom they will be writing a letter. (You can have them sign their letters or keep their identities secret for a while.)

◆ Set up some ground rules about language, content, etc. You will know what is appropriate for your class.

◆ Pass out copies of "Writing a Letter" and have students work independently.

◆ Encourage students to answer the letters they receive, paying attention to questions that were asked and commenting on the information that was given.

To Simplify:

Have students work with aides or parent volunteers.

To Expand:

Start corresponding with pen pals from different states or even different countries.

Evaluation and Processing:

Ask students: How are letters different from oral conversation? Are they fun to receive? Are they as much fun to write? Do you feel as if you know your correspondent better than you did before? Why? Do you plan to keep writing letters when this activity is over?

Segment Seven—Lesson Eight *(cont.)*

Conversation/Letter Writing

Writing a Letter

Writing a letter should be fun. Follow these easy suggestions:

1. Try to write the way you talk. In a letter to a friend, you do not need to worry about things like complete sentences.

2. Give some interesting information about what you have been doing and what you plan to do in the near future.

3. Ask questions. Then your correspondent will have more to say when answering your letter. When you are answering a letter, do not forget to answer the questions that were asked.

4. If you are artistic (or even if you are not), illustrate your letter with little pictures and/or designs.

Try a short letter on the lines below.

_____

_____

_____

_____

_____

_____

_____

_____

_____

_____

_____

_____

_____

Interpersonal

Segment Seven—Lesson Nine

Sharing Translations

Purpose: to give students the opportunity to share their various translations and activity sheets

Skills: knowledge, comprehension, application, analysis, synthesis, and evaluation

Intelligences: Potentially all may be involved.

Materials:

- individual student folders

Procedures:

◆ Invite students to share their translations and activity sheets from this segment.

◆ Allow enough time for presentations and positive acknowledgements of their efforts.

To Simplify:

Allow students to work with an aide or helper, if they wish.

To Expand:

Encourage students to use the techniques they learned in this segment on future assignments.

Evaluation and Processing:

This activity is actually an evaluation and processing of the entire segment.

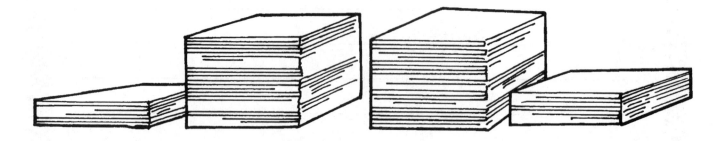

Segment Eight—Nine Lessons

From the Middle of May Through the First Week of June

During the eighth and final segment of this minicurriculum, students will have their last experience with archetypal examples of the intelligences, as we consider the intrapersonal.

Intrapersonal means tending to turn inward to explore one's own thoughts and feelings—reflecting, daydreaming, imagining, and planning for the future. People with this kind of intelligence enjoy working alone, reading, and engaging in self-analysis. They are usually self-directed and self-confident. They possess great self-esteem and tend to have strong opinions on controversial issues.

The topics in this segment include suggestions for supplying students with opportunities to engage in archetypal examples of intrapersonal intelligence, such as time management, journaling, and self-talk. They will also be encouraged to try out some of the tools they need in order to successfully manage this type of intelligence, including learning to be assertive rather than aggressive and self-disciplined rather than simply wishful.

The topics selected for this segment are listed below. Brief descriptions and/or explanations follow for your convenience. You may wish to refresh your own familiarity with them. You should, of course, feel free to substitute or add your own favorite topics. If this is "your" intelligence, you will have favorite topics that make this area come alive for you.

1. Reading for Pleasure

2. Journaling

3. Self-Talk

4. Time Management

5. Being Assertive

6. Daydreaming

7. Becoming Self-Disciplined

8. Planning for the Future

9. Sharing Translations

Calendars for Segment Eight

Directions: Use the calendars below to plan when you would like to do the nine lessons of this segment. The lessons are listed on the previous page. The highlighted weeks are the time periods which are suggested.

May

M	T	W	T	F
		Segment Eight		
		Segment Eight		

June

M	T	W	T	F
		Segment Eight		

Segment Eight

References

Intrapersonal experiences are hard to observe in other people because, by definition, they are things that go on inside. Translations of the experiences can work really well, as long as the experiences themselves are respected as being private and as belonging to the person who had them.

1. Reading for Pleasure

Reading for pleasure is a pursuit favored by people with intrapersonal intelligence because it allows them to be alone, to reflect, and to daydream.

When you are reading for pleasure, you can choose books that . . .

- are a little too easy for you so you can read quickly and without stress

- are a little too hard for you because no one else needs to know if you have difficulty

- deal with a subject you know a lot about so that you can judge what the author has to say

- deal with a subject that is totally new to you so that you can learn

- are written in a variety of styles, because if you do not like one, you can always put it down and pick up another.

2. Journaling

Keeping a journal or a diary is a great way to cultivate your intrapersonal intelligence. A journal is a written record of one's thoughts, feelings, and experiences. Some people write in their journals every day without fail. Some people write only occasionally when they have important things to say.

The most important thing about a real journal is that it is private. No one should ever read another person's journal without permission. Journals written at school are probably not real journals. They are usually writing exercises that will probably be read for assessment purposes. This is fine as long as one realizes that it is not the same as the kind of journal one would write if he or she were sure no one was going to read it.

Journals, whether they are school assignments or personal journals, can help people to sort out and clarify their thoughts. Just putting one's thoughts down on paper gives them a fresh perspective.

Segment Eight (cont.)

References (cont.)

3. Self-Talk

What in the world is self-talk? How does it differ from writing in a journal or simply thinking, for that matter?

Journaling is done on purpose, of course, and so is thinking. Self-talk, however, is the unending spontaneous conversation that goes on inside everyone's head. Very often it is between a person's creative side and his or her practical side. For example:

> **Creative Side:** I think I'll set up my easel and paint today . . .
>
> **Practical Side:** and have to clean up all that mess.
>
> **CS:** It wasn't so bad last time.
>
> **PS:** It took hours! That blue sweater still has a spot on it.
>
> **CS:** But Pat really liked the painting.
>
> **PS:** I wonder where it is. I haven't seen it lately.

Self-talk can also be extremely negative. It is the voice that says, "You are really stupid!" when you make a mistake. Or, when you spend all your birthday money on a great new shirt and are planning to look nice at school the next day, it says, "Why even bother? You always make a mess of yourself!"

The good news is that you can learn to turn negative self-talk into positive self-talk.

4. Time Management

Time management is simply having the skills necessary to manage your time without missing deadlines, feeling constant panic, or never being able to do anything just for fun.

In order to manage your time, you must know:

- how much time you have
- what you have to do
- when it has to be done

Your most important tool in time management is one calendar! (More than one is worse than none.) However, the calendar will not work by itself. You have to write things on it.

Segment Eight (cont.)

References (cont.)

5. Being Assertive

If you are assertive, you simply stick up for yourself, your ideas, and your rights without getting angry.

If you want to do something, you can say "yes." If you do not want to do something, you can say "no."

There are some techniques you can learn so that your assertiveness will not offend other people.

6. Daydreaming

Daydreaming, imagining, and pretending are all important parts of intrapersonal intelligence. This is where creativity begins.

It is also possible to become so good at this intrapersonal talent that one can use it as a kind of mental programming. Many athletes practice their physical skills in their minds before they ever perform them with their bodies. Greg Louganis, the Olympic gold medalist, always went through every twist and turn of his dives, over and over, before getting on the diving board. Wayne Gretzky, the well-known ice hockey player, has said that he sees the puck going into the net before he ever hits it. Dwight Stone, the famous high jumper, was one of the first to practice his jumps in his head.

You do not have to be an Olympic or professional athlete to use this technique. You do not even have to be an athlete. It works in everyday life just as well. You can practice being calm during a test before you ever take it by practicing in your mind. You can practice getting along with your teacher or being nice to your sister. The more you use this technique, the better you will get at it.

7. Becoming Self-Disciplined

People with intrapersonal intelligence sometimes tend to be "wishful thinkers." They spend so much time wishing and dreaming that they do not always get around to putting their dreams into action. Although it is true that you cannot plan the action without first having the dream, you cannot realize the dream without acting on it. Even the mental programming discussed in the last activity is not an end in itself. The successfully executed action is the real goal.

Segment Eight *(cont.)*

References *(cont.)*

7. Becoming Self-Disciplined *(cont.)*

One way to develop self-discipline is to find ways to put your dreams into action. If you see yourself as fit and healthy and practicing a lifestyle that includes exercise, the next step is to set up an exercise program that fits into your time management calendar. Then, actually begin to exercise. If you see yourself as getting all A's on your next report card, the next step is to plan a study schedule that you can stick to and then actually crack a book.

8. Planning for the Future

Planning for the future is the next step.

You already know how to . . .

- replace negative self-talk with positive self-talk

- manage your time

- be assertive

You already can . . .

- program your daydreaming

- turn your dreams into reality by being self-disciplined

Now you can plan for the future by . . .

- comparing your dreams with reality

- considering your options

- learning the steps to take

- making progress one step at a time

9. Sharing Translations

Intrapersonal

Segment Eight—Lesson One

Reading for Pleasure

Purpose: to give students a new perspective at reading for pleasure

Skills: knowledge, comprehension, application, analysis, synthesis, and evaluation

Intelligences: Potentially all may be involved.

Materials:

- copies of "My Private Reading Record," one for each student

- copies of "Translating the Experience," one per book read for each student

Procedures:

- ◆ Have students review the definition of intrapersonal intelligence.
- ◆ Introduce this experience by giving a brief overview of reading for pleasure. (See the "References" section.)
- ◆ Discuss with students the special difficulty associated with intrapersonal experiences, especially in school: If they stay purely intrapersonal, no one will know anything about them. Translation into another intelligence is particularly important for an intrapersonal experience.
- ◆ Have students go to the library and choose something to read. Do not suggest books or comment on their choices. Give them as much time as possible to read. If they need to exchange their books for others, that is fine.
- ◆ Pass out copies of "My Private Reading Record" and ask the students to write down the titles, authors, and types of books they read during this nine-lesson segment.
- ◆ Each time students finish a book, ask them to complete "Translating the Experience" and put it in their folders.
- ◆ Save all of these translations to share on the last day of this segment.

To Simplify:

Most intrapersonal experiences are standard for everyone.

To Expand:

Most intrapersonal experiences are standard for everyone.

Evaluation and Processing:

This experience carries over through the entire nine-lesson segment.

Segment Eight—Lesson One *(cont.)*

Reading for Pleasure

Name _____

My Private Reading Record

After reading a book, fill in a line on the chart below. To rate the book, consider how much you enjoyed reading it. Use a point system of 1 through 10, 10 being the best, or make up your own rating system.

Title	Author	Type	Rating

Segment Eight—Lesson One *(cont.)*

Reading for Pleasure

Translating the Experience (Complete one for each book you read.)

Think about the experience you just had. It was an intrapersonal experience. You read a book to yourself for pleasure. It was also another kind of experience. Which other intelligence was involved?

Think about your reaction to the experience. Can you translate your reaction into still another one of the intelligences? Which intelligence?

_____

_____

_____

What materials, if any, will you need?

_____   _____

_____   _____

_____   _____

Will you need time to prepare your translation? How much?

_____

How will you share your translation with the class?

_____

_____

_____

_____

_____

_____

Intrapersonal

Segment Eight—Lesson Two

Journaling

Purpose: to give students the experience of keeping a journal

Skills: knowledge, comprehension, application, analysis, synthesis, and evaluation

Intelligences: Potentially all may be involved.

Materials:

- copies of "Private Journal Pages," five for each student
- copies of "Translating the Experience," one for each student

Procedures:

◆ Have students review the definition of intrapersonal intelligence.

◆ Introduce this experience by giving a brief overview of keeping a journal. (See the "References" section.)

◆ Tell students they will be keeping a private journal at home for five days. They will be taking home enough journal pages for that length of time. They will never have to bring their journal pages back to school.

◆ At the end of a week, pass out the page entitled "Translating the Experience" for students to complete.

◆ Use these sheets for discussion during Evaluation and Processing and then place them in the students' folders.

To Simplify:

Most intrapersonal experiences are standard for everyone.

To Expand:

Most intrapersonal experiences are standard for everyone.

Evaluation and Processing:

Although students will not be expected to discuss their journals, they may want to discuss "Translating the Experience." They may also be willing to discuss whether or not they plan to continue keeping a journal and why or why not.

Segment Eight—Lesson Two (cont.)

Journaling

Private Journal Pages

Write as little or as much as you want every day for five days.

Segment Eight—Lesson Two *(cont.)*

Journaling

Translating the Experience

Think about the experience you just had. It was an intrapersonal experience. You wrote, just for yourself, in a journal. It was also another kind of experience. Which other intelligence was involved? _____

Think about your reaction to the experience. Can you translate your reaction into still another one of the intelligences? Which intelligence? _____

_____

Which intelligence will you use to translate your experience?

_____

What materials, if any, will you need?

_____   _____

_____   _____

_____

Will you need time to prepare your translation? How much?

_____

How will you share your translation with the class?

_____

_____

_____

_____

_____

_____

My Journal by Carlos

Intrapersonal

Segment Eight—Lesson Three

Self-Talk

Purpose: to give students the experience of controlling negative self-talk

Skills: knowledge, comprehension, application, analysis, synthesis, and evaluation

Intelligences: Potentially all may be involved.

Materials:

- copies of "Positive Self-Talk," one for each student
- copies of "Translating the Experience," one for each student

Procedures:

◆ Have students review the definition of intrapersonal intelligence.

◆ Introduce this experience by giving a brief overview of self-talk. (See the "References" section.)

◆ Students who have heard "talking to one's self" compared to being crazy will be relieved to hear that everybody does it. Discuss this as a group.

◆ Tell students that they will be learning to react to and stop their own negative self-talk by replacing it with positive self-talk.

◆ Pass out "Positive Self-Talk" and ask students to follow the directions and complete the sheet

◆ Ask students to fill out the page entitled "Translating the Experience" after trying to self-talk positively for a day or two.

◆ Use these sheets for discussion during Evaluation and Processing and then place them in the students folders.

To Simplify:

Most intrapersonal experiences are standard for everyone.

To Expand:

Most intrapersonal experiences are standard for everyone.

Evaluation and Processing:

Although students will not be expected to discuss their own negative and positive self-talk, they may want to discuss "Translating the Experience." They may also be willing to discuss whether or not they plan to continue the practice of positive self-talk and why or why not.

Segment Eight—Lesson Three *(cont.)*

Self-Talk

Positive Self-Talk

Negative self-talk can be turned into positive self-talk by always . . .

- being aware of that negative voice in your head
- responding to the negative talk
- creating positive self-talk that is exactly its opposite
- letting your positive self-voice be sure of itself and full of energy

---

The opposite of "You are really stupid!" is "You are really smart!" not "You're okay."

The opposite of "You were born ugly!" is "You were born good-looking!" not "You look all right."

What negative remark do you most often hear in your head?

_____

_____

_____

Write its exact opposite on the lines below.

_____

_____

_____

Practice saying it to yourself in the mirror. Say it often during the day. Keep a tally of how many times you say it:

Segment Eight—Lesson Three *(cont.)*

Self-Talk

Translating the Experience

Think about the experience you just had. It was an intrapersonal experience. You participated in controlling your own negative self-talk. It was also another kind of experience. Which other intelligence was involved?

Think about your reaction to the experience. Can you translate your reaction into still another one of the intelligences? Which intelligence?

Which intelligence will you use to translate your experience?

_____

What materials, if any, will you need?

_____   _____

_____   _____

_____   _____

Will you need time to prepare your translation? How much?

_____

How will you share your translation with the class?

_____

_____

_____

_____

_____

_____

_____

_____

Good Job!

Intrapersonal

Segment Eight—Lesson Four

Time Management

Purpose: to give students experience in managing their own time

Skills: knowledge, comprehension, application, analysis, synthesis, and evaluation

Intelligences: intrapersonal, verbal/linguistic, visual/spatial

Materials:

- copies of the "Calendar," one for each student, plus extras
- assorted school, class, and sports schedules
- copies of "Translating the Experience," one for each student

Procedures:

◆ Have students review the definition of intrapersonal intelligence.

◆ Introduce this experience by giving a brief overview of time management. (See the "References" section.)

◆ Pass out a copy of the "Calendar" to each student. Pass out copies of assorted school, class, and sports schedules (holidays, reports, presentations, practices, etc.) and have students fill in their calendars.

◆ Have students think of things that are important at home, such as family and personal events and commitments (everything from birthdays and weddings to time for reading a book). Have them block these in on their calendars.

◆ Have students take a look at their calendars and the time they have left after allowing for everything that needs to be done. Do they have too much free time or too little? This is a personal and private judgment. No one should have to discuss it, but they do need to consider it.

◆ Have students complete the page entitled "Translating the Experience."

◆ Use these sheets for discussion during Evaluation and Processing and then place them in the students' folders.

To Simplify:

Most intrapersonal experiences are standard for everyone.

To Expand:

Most intrapersonal experiences are standard for everyone.

Evaluation and Processing:

Although students will not be expected to discuss their own time management, they may want to discuss "Translating the Experience." They may also be willing to discuss whether or not they plan to continue trying to manage their time.

Segment Eight—Lesson Four *(cont.)*

Time Management

_____
(month)

In order to manage your time, you must know how much time you have, what you have to do, and when it has to be done. This calendar will help you organize your time.

Sunday	Monday	Tuesday	Wednesday	Thursday	Friday	Saturday

Segment Eight—Lesson Four *(cont.)*

Time Management

Translating the Experience

Look at a blank copy of the calendar. How do you feel about having that much unstructured time? Translate your feelings into a visual/spatial experience by drawing a picture of how you feel.

Look at the calendar page you just filled in. How do you feel about having that much planned time? Draw a picture of how you feel.

Intrapersonal

Segment Eight—Lesson Five

Being Assertive

Purpose: to give students information about assertiveness techniques

Skills: knowledge, comprehension, application, analysis, synthesis, and evaluation

Intelligences: Potentially all may be involved.

Materials:

- copies of "Assertiveness Techniques," one for each student, plus extras

- copies of "Translating the Experience," one for each student

Procedures:

◆ Have students review the definition of intrapersonal intelligence.

◆ Introduce this experience by giving a brief overview of being assertive. (See the "References" section.)

◆ Pass out a copy of "Assertiveness Techniques" to each student. Read it together. Allow students to discuss the techniques if they want to.

◆ Ask students to consider how assertiveness techniques relate to time management. Discuss.

◆ Have students work individually to complete "Assertiveness Techniques."

◆ Have students complete the page entitled "Translating the Experience."

◆ Use these sheets for discussion during Evaluation and Processing and then place them in the students' folders.

To Simplify:

Most intrapersonal experiences are standard for everyone.

To Expand:

Most intrapersonal experiences are standard for everyone.

Evaluation and Processing:

Although students will not be expected to discuss their use of assertiveness techniques, they may want to discuss "Translating the Experience." They may also be willing to discuss whether or not they plan to put any of the assertiveness techniques into action.

Segment Eight—Lesson Five *(cont.)*

Being Assertive

Assertiveness Techniques

Assertiveness techniques make it possible for you to do what you want without making other people feel bad.

When someone asks you to do something that you do not have time for and you do not want to hurt that person's feelings, you could say,

- "Let me check my calendar, and I'll get back to you."

(This is where assertiveness techniques and time management techniques relate to one another.)

When someone asks you to do something that you do not want to do and you do not want that person to think you are judging him or her, you could say,

- "My parents would ground me for life!"

Write your own answers to these requests:

1. Will you help with the car wash on Saturday?

   _____

   _____

2. Will you come to the party I'm having while my parents are away?

   _____

   _____

3. There is going to be a fight in the park after school. Want to watch?

   _____

   _____

4. Can you take part in the talent show for the assembly next Friday?

   _____

   _____

   _____

Segment Eight—Lesson Five (cont.)

Being Assertive

Translating the Experience

Think about the experience you just had. It was an intrapersonal experience. You were thinking of assertive answers to requests. It was also another kind of experience. Which other intelligence was involved?

Think about your reaction to the experience. Can you translate your reaction into still another one of the intelligences? Which intelligence?

Which intelligence will you use to translate your experience?

_____

What materials, if any, will you need?

_____   _____

_____   _____

_____   _____

Will you need time to prepare your translation? How much?

_____

How will you share your translation with the class?

_____

_____

_____

_____

_____

_____

_____

Intrapersonal

Segment Eight—Lesson Six

Daydreaming

Purpose: to give students information about mental rehearsals

Skills: knowledge, comprehension, application, analysis, synthesis, and evaluation

Intelligences: Potentially all may be involved.

Materials:

- copies of "Mental Rehearsals," one for each student, plus extras

- copies of "Translating the Experience," one for each student

Procedures:

◆ Have students review the definition of intrapersonal intelligence.

◆ Introduce this experience by giving a brief overview of daydreaming and mental rehearsal. (See the "References" section.)

◆ Pass out a copy of "Mental Rehearsals" to each student. Read it together. Allow students to discuss the technique if they want to.

◆ Have students work individually to complete "Mental Rehearsals."

◆ Have students complete the page entitled "Translating the Experience" after a week has passed.

◆ Use these sheets for discussion during Evaluation and Processing and then place them in the students' folders.

To Simplify:

Most intrapersonal experiences are standard for everyone.

To Expand:

Most intrapersonal experiences are standard for everyone.

Evaluation and Processing:

Although students will not be expected to discuss their use of mental rehearsal techniques, they may want to discuss "Translating the Experience." They may also be willing to discuss whether or not they plan to put any of the mental rehearsal techniques into action.

Segment Eight—Lesson Six *(cont.)*

Daydreaming

Mental Rehearsals

Mental rehearsal techniques make it possible for you to practice doing something without moving a muscle. You stay inside your own head all of the time. No one else needs to know what you are doing.

Think of an activity that is part of your everyday life, something you do automatically. It could be putting on a jacket. It could be pouring cereal into a bowl and adding milk.

See yourself, in slow motion, doing this activity. On a piece of scratch paper, write it down, step by step, in great detail. Go over it a few times until you are sure you have all of the steps.

Now think of something you want to do really well, for example, hit a ball, do a dance step, write neatly and legibly, or say something pleasant when you meet a friend. Rehearse whatever it is mentally until you can see every step. Write the steps on the lines below.

Rehearse these steps inside your head at least three times a day. Read them over before you start rehearsing so that you do not miss any steps. After a week, try whatever you have been rehearsing in real life and see what happens. Is there any change? Are you better at it?

_____

_____

_____

_____

_____

_____

_____

_____

Segment Eight—Lesson Six *(cont.)*

Daydreaming

Translating the Experience

Think about the experience you just had. It began as an intrapersonal experience. You were doing something inside your own head. At the end you translated it into another kind of experience. Which intelligence were you using at the end?

Think about your reaction to the experience. Can you translate your reaction into still another one of the intelligences? Which intelligence?

If you thought of more than one, which of these intelligences will you use to translate your experience?

_____

_____

What materials, if any, will you need?

_____   _____

_____   _____

_____   _____

Will you need time to prepare your translation? How much?

_____

How will you share your translation with the class?

_____

_____

_____

_____

_____

_____

Intrapersonal

Segment Eight-Lesson Seven

Becoming Self-Disciplined

Purpose: to give students information about cultivating self-discipline

Skills: knowledge, comprehension, application, analysis, synthesis, and evaluation

Intelligences: Potentially all may be involved.

Materials:

- copies of "From Dream to Reality," one for each student, plus extras

- copies of "Translating the Experience," one for each student

Procedures:

◆ Have students review the definition of intrapersonal intelligence.

◆ Introduce this experience by giving a brief overview on becoming self-disciplined. (See the "References" section.)

◆ Pass out a copy of "From Dream to Reality" to each student. Read it together. Allow students to discuss the process if they want to.

◆ Have students work individually to complete "From Dream to Reality."

◆ Have students complete the page entitled "Translating the Experience."

◆ Use these sheets for discussion during Evaluation and Processing and then place them in the students' folders.

To Simplify:

Most intrapersonal experiences are standard for everyone.

To Expand:

Most intrapersonal experiences are standard for everyone.

Evaluation and Processing:

Although students will not be expected to discuss their process of becoming self-disciplined, they may want to discuss "Translating the Experience." They may also be willing to discuss whether or not they plan to try any of the ideas they mapped out.

Segment Eight—Lesson Seven

Becoming Self-Disciplined

From Dream to Reality

Moving from dream to reality is a lot easier than it sounds, if you know how.

First, you need to have a picture in your mind of what you want (the dream).

Second, you need go through a step-by-step rehearsal (the plan).

Third, you need to go ahead and try it (the reality).

The Dream: _____

_____

_____

The Plan: _____

_____

_____

_____

_____

_____

The Reality: _____

_____

_____

_____

_____

I will put this plan into action on _____

_____

(signature)

Segment Eight—Lesson Seven *(cont.)*

Becoming Self-Disciplined

Translating the Experience

This started out as an intrapersonal experience. It is your own private dream and your own private plan. When you turn the dream and the plan into reality, it will be an automatic translation. The kind(s) of intelligence(s) involved will depend on the dream and the plan you started with.

Think about your reaction to the experience. Can you translate your reaction into still another one of the intelligences? Which intelligence?

If you thought of more than one, which of these intelligences will you use to translate your experience?

_____

_____

What materials, if any, will you need?

_____   _____

_____   _____

_____   _____

Will you need time to prepare your translation? How much?

_____

How will you share your translation with the class?

_____

_____

_____

_____

_____

Dream
↓
Plan
↓
Reality

Intrapersonal

Segment Eight—Lesson Eight

Planning for the Future

Purpose: to give students information about planning for the future

Skills: knowledge, comprehension, application, analysis, synthesis, and evaluation

Intelligences: Potentially all may be involved.

Materials:

- copies of "Here Comes the Future!," both pages, one set for each student

- copies of "Translating the Experience," one for each student

Procedures:

◆ Have students review the definition of intrapersonal intelligence.

◆ Introduce this experience by giving a brief overview of planning for the future. (See the "References" section.)

◆ Pass out a copy of "Here Comes the Future!" to each student. Read it together. Allow students to discuss the process if they want to.

◆ Have students work individually to complete "Here Comes the Future!"

◆ Have students complete the page entitled "Translating the Experience."

◆ Use these sheets for discussion during Evaluation and Processing and then place them in the students' folders.

To Simplify:

Most intrapersonal experiences are standard for everyone.

To Expand:

Most intrapersonal experiences are standard for everyone.

Evaluation and Processing:

Although students will not be expected to discuss their plans for the future, they may want to discuss "Translating the Experience." They may also be willing to discuss whether or not they plan to try any of the ideas they mapped out.

Segment Eight—Lesson Eight *(cont.)*

Planning for the Future

Here Comes the Future!

Planning for the future can be done by following these simple steps:

- First, compare your dreams with reality.
- Second, consider your options.
- Third, learn the steps to take.
- Fourth, make progress one step at a time.

Let's take the case of planning for a career (what you want to do when you grow up).

1. Compare your dream with reality.

(For example, if you faint at the sight of blood, think twice about being a doctor. If everyone in your family is short, you probably will not be tall enough for the NBA. On the other hand, if you like little children and you love to learn, you might consider being a teacher.)

Dream: _____

_____

Reality: _____

_____

2. Consider your options.

(What are the different ways you could achieve this goal? If you will need to go to college, how will you pay for it? Are there community colleges near where you live? Can you get a job that will give you some experience in your career area so you can see if you really like it?)

Option 1: _____

_____

Option 2: _____

_____

Option 3: _____

_____

Segment Eight—Lesson Eight *(cont.)*

Planning for the Future

Here Comes the Future! *(cont.)*

3. Learn the steps to take.

(Talk to someone in the field that you are considering and find out how to reach your career goal. That way, you will not waste time doing unnecessary things or skipping some really important steps.)

Step 1:_____

_____

Step 2:_____

_____

Step 3:_____

_____

Step 4:_____

_____

Step 5:_____

_____

4. Make progress one step at a time.

(Is there anything you can do now? Could you send for information about colleges? You could be learning about their requirements. Could you get information from some professional organizations? Could you find out what scholarships are available and what you would have to do to qualify?)

_____

_____

_____

_____

Segment Eight—Lesson Eight (cont.)

Planning for the Future

Translating the Experience

This started out as an intrapersonal experience. It is your own plan for the future. As you start to take steps towards your goal, there will be an automatic translation. The kind(s) of intelligence(s) involved will depend on the dream and the plan you started with.

What if you change your mind? Then you simply go back to the intrapersonal part of your planning process and start over.

Think about your reaction to the experience. Can you translate your reaction into still another one of the intelligences? Which intelligence?

If you thought of more than one, which of these intelligences will you use to translate your experience?

_____

_____

What materials, if any, will you need?

_____   _____

_____   _____

_____   _____

Will you need time to prepare your translation? How much?

_____

How will you share your translation with the class?

_____

_____

_____

_____

_____

Intrapersonal

Segment Eight—Lesson Nine

Sharing Translations

Purpose: to give students the opportunity to share their various translations and activity sheets

Skills: knowledge, comprehension, application, analysis, synthesis, and evaluation

Intelligences: Potentially all may be involved.

Materials:

- individual student folders

Procedures:

◆ Invite students to share their translations and activity sheets from this segment.

◆ Allow time for presentations and positive acknowledgements of their efforts.

To Simplify:

Allow students to work with an aide or helper, if they wish.

To Expand:

Encourage students to use the techniques they learned in this segment on future assignments.

Evaluation and Processing:

This activity is actually an evaluation and processing of the entire segment.

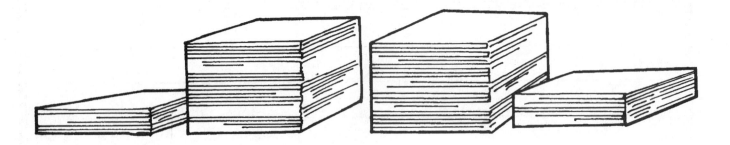